First published in Great Britain in 2026 by Hamlyn, an imprint of Octopus Publishing Group Ltd, Carmelite House, 50 Victoria Embankment London EC4Y 0DZ www.octopusbooks.co.uk

An Hachette UK Company www.hachette.co.uk

The authorized representative in the EEA is Hachette Ireland, 8 Castlecourt Centre, Dublin 15, D15 XTP3, Ireland (email: info@hbgi.ie)

Distributed in the US by Hachette Book Group, 1290 Avenue of the Americas, 4th and 5th Floors, New York, NY 10104

Distributed in Canada by Canadian Manda Group, 664 Annette St., Toronto, Ontario, Canada M6S 2C8

ISBN 978-0-60064-013-4
eISBN 978-0-60064-019-6

A CIP catalogue record for this book is available from the British Library.

Printed and bound in Great Britian.

10 9 8 7 6 5 4 3 2 1

Publisher: Lucy Pessell
Senior Designer: Alicia House
Senior Project Editor: Katie Button
Assistant Editor: Samina Rahman
Production Manager: Allison Gonsalves

This FSC® label means that materials used for the product have been responsibly sourced.

MIX
Paper | Supporting responsible forestry
FSC® C104740

RECIPES FOR
Savoury Bakes

A Collection of Timeless
and Trusted Recipes

hamlyn

Contents

Introduction

Who can resist the buttery aroma of pastry fresh from the oven or the smoky-sweet tang of toasted rosemary and bubbling Gruyère?

Hold the sugar and pass the salt – here are over 75 recipes for irresistible cheesy, herby, creamy and spicy bakes.

From cornbreads and flatbreads to samosas and bhajis, tiny tarts and picnic pies to sensational soufflés and moreish muffins, there's plenty of inspiration for decadent date nights, midweek suppers and comforting lunches. You'll find classics such as sausage rolls and French onion tarts but also fun twists such as cheese and matcha scones and a vegan Wellington to widen your repertoire.

Many of the recipes in this book start with shortcrust pastry and there's a recipe in The Basics section overleaf – it's a great, versatile pastry that's easy to make and which you can customise to suit your bake. Consider keeping a supply of shop-bought or homemade pastry in the freezer – just remember to take it out in plenty of time so that the pastry can defrost at room temperature.

The
Basics

Shortcrust Pastry

MAKES 470 g (15 oz)

250 g (8 oz) plain flour
125 g (4 oz) half butter and
half white vegetable fat or
lard, or all butter, diced

2½–3 tablespoons cold water
salt

Add the flour and a pinch of salt to a large mixing bowl. Add the fats and rub them into the flour with your fingertips or use a freestanding electric mixer until the mixture resembles fine crumbs.

Gradually mix in just enough water – allowing 1 teaspoon per 25 g (1 oz) of flour – to enable the crumbs to be squeezed together to form a soft but not sticky dough.

Knead very lightly until smooth, then chill in the fridge for 30 minutes.

Roll out on a lightly floured surface and use to line a tart case or to top a pie.

For flavour variations, try adding 1 teaspoon of English mustard powder, fresh chopped herbs such as rosemary, or 40 g (1½ oz) of freshly grated Parmesan or mature Cheddar.

Gluten-free pastry

If you have an intolerance to gluten, rice flour or wheat-free bread flour can be used instead of wheat flour. The pastry is quite crumbly, so does require careful handling; it can either be rolled out between two sheets of clingfilm or pressed directly into a greased tin. If the pastry does crack, simply press it back together again or patch with extra pieces of pastry, sticking in place with beaten egg, milk or water.

Ready-made pastry

When using puff pastry, try to keep an even pressure when rolling it out so that the finished pie will rise evenly. Sprinkle the work surface only very lightly with flour – just enough that it won't stick. Filo pastry can dry out very quickly as the sheets are wafer thin. If shaping tiny boureks, unfold the pastry, but keep the remaining stack covered with clingfilm or a teatowel and try to use it as quickly as possible.

Baking blind

This term simply means to bake the tart case empty.

Prick the base of the pastry case with a fork. Chill for 15 minutes to allow the pastry to 'relax'; this will help to minimize shrinkage during baking.

Line the tart case with a piece of crumpled greaseproof or nonstick baking paper that is large enough to cover the base and sides of the tart.

Add a generous layer of baking beans if you have them, or otherwise use some dried rice or pulses.

Put the tart on a baking sheet and bake in a preheated oven, 190°C (375°F), Gas Mark 5, for 10–15 minutes for a large tart, 8–10 minutes for individual tarts and 5 minutes for mini muffin-sized tarts, until the case is just set. Carefully lift the paper and beans out of the tart case and cook empty for 5 minutes for a large tart, 4–5 minutes for individual tarts and 2–3 minutes for mini muffin-sized tarts, until the base is dry and crisp and the top edges of the tart are pale golden.

Lining a pastry case

A loose-bottomed tart tin makes it easy to remove the finished tart after baking. Roll out the pastry you are using on a lightly floured surface. Lift it over a rolling pin and drape into the tin.

Press over the base and up the sides of the tin with your fingertips, taking care where the sides meet the base.

Trim off the excess pastry with a knife a little above the top of the tin to allow for shrinkage.

Decorating

Flute the edges by pressing two fingers onto the pie edge, then make small cuts with a knife between them to create a scalloped edge. Repeat all the way around the pie. Brush the pie with a little beaten egg or milk to glaze it.

To decorate with pastry leaves, reroll the pastry trimmings and then cut out small diamond shapes. Mark veins with the knife, then position on the pie. Glaze the decorations with a little more beaten egg or milk before baking.

Small Plates & Sides

Onion & Goats' Cheese Tart

SERVES 8
PREPARATION TIME 20 minutes + cooling
COOKING TIME 20–25 minutes

40 g (1½ oz) butter
500 g (1 lb) onions,
    thinly sliced
2 garlic cloves, crushed
1 tablespoon chopped thyme

350 g (12 oz) ready-made puff
    pastry, defrosted if frozen
200 g (7 oz) soft goats' cheese,
    crumbled or diced
salt and black pepper

Melt the butter in a frying pan, add the onions, garlic and thyme and cook over a medium heat, stirring occasionally, for 20–25 minutes until soft and golden. Leave to cool.

Roll the pastry out and lay it on a baking sheet.

Spread the onion mixture over the pastry, leaving a 1 cm (½ inch) border. Scatter over the goats' cheese and bake for 20–25 minutes until the pastry is puffed up and the cheese is golden. Leave to cool slightly and serve warm.

Spiced Pear & Stilton Tarts with Watercress

MAKES 4
PREPARATION TIME 15 minutes
COOKING TIME 16–18 minutes

300 g (10 oz) ready-made puff
    pastry, defrosted if frozen
flour, for dusting
25 g (1 oz) butter, melted, plus
    extra for greasing
¼ teaspoon ground cloves
pinch of ground allspice
¼ teaspoon ground black
    pepper
2 ripe but firm pears, peeled,
    cored and sliced

75 g (3 oz) Stilton
25 g (1 oz) walnut pieces
1 teaspoon thyme leaves
1 red chilli, deseeded and
    chopped (optional)

TO SERVE
watercress
maple syrup

Lightly grease a baking sheet. Roll out the pastry on a lightly floured work surface to the thickness of about 3 mm (⅛ inch). Using a 12 cm (5 inch) saucer as a template, cut out 4 circles and place them on the prepared baking sheet.

Brush the circles with the melted butter and, using the tip of a sharp knife and a slightly smaller saucer, score a 1 cm (½ inch) border around the edge of each one. Bake in a preheated oven, 200°C (400°F), Gas Mark 6, for about 8 minutes, until pale golden in colour.

Meanwhile, combine the cloves, allspice and pepper in a bowl.

Remove the pastries from the oven and arrange the pear slices on them, keeping within the border. Dust lightly with the spices, then crumble over the Stilton and sprinkle with the walnuts and thyme leaves. Dot with the chilli, if using.

Return the pastries to the oven for a further 8–10 minutes, until crisp and golden.

Serve with a handful of watercress leaves drizzled with a little maple syrup.

Parmesan & Tomato Tarts

MAKES 24
PREPARATION TIME 30 minutes + chilling
COOKING TIME 18–20 minutes

FOR THE PASTRY
175 g (6 oz) plain flour, plus
    extra for dusting
75 g (3 oz) butter, diced, plus
    extra for greasing
2 tablespoons chopped basil
2 tablespoons cold water
salt and pepper

FOR THE FILLING
2 eggs
150 ml (¼ pint) milk
50 g (2 oz) Parmesan,
    finely grated
3 spring onions, finely
    chopped
12 cherry tomatoes, halved
salt and pepper
tiny basil leaves, to garnish

Make the pastry. Add the flour, a little salt and pepper and the butter to a mixing bowl, then rub in the butter with your fingertips or using an electric mixer until you have fine crumbs. Add the basil, then mix in enough water to form a soft but not sticky dough.

Knead the pastry lightly, then roll it out thinly on a lightly floured surface. Stamp out 24 x 6 cm (2½ inch) circles with a plain cutter, then press into the greased holes of two 12-cup mini muffin tins, rerolling the trimmings as needed. Chill for 15 minutes.

Make the filling. Fork the eggs and milk together in a bowl. Add the Parmesan, spring onions and a little salt and pepper and mix well. Spoon into the pastry cases, then add a tomato half to each one.

Bake in a preheated oven, 180°C (350°F), Gas Mark 4, for 18–20 minutes until golden and the filling is just set. Leave to stand for 10 minutes, then loosen the edges of the tarts and remove from the tins. Garnish with tiny basil leaves just before serving.

Onion &
Chorizo Tarts

MAKES 12
PREPARATION TIME 30 minutes + chilling
COOKING TIME 30–35 minutes

1 quantity all-butter
  shortcrust pastry
  (see page 7)
flour, for dusting
25 g (1 oz) butter, plus extra
  for greasing
1 onion, thinly sliced
100 g (3½ oz) chorizo, diced

4 eggs
200 ml (7 fl oz) milk
125 g (4 oz) Gruyère,
  finely grated
a few fresh thyme leaves
salt and pepper

Roll the pastry out thinly on a lightly floured surface, then stamp out 12 x 10 cm (4 inch) circles with a plain cutter, and press into the greased holes of a 12-section muffin tin. Reroll the pastry trimmings as needed. Chill for 15 minutes.

Heat the butter in a frying pan, add the onion and chorizo and fry until the onion has softened and just beginning to brown.

Add the eggs and milk to a large wide-necked jug, and fork together until just well combined. Add the cheese, thyme and seasoning and mix together. Divide the mixture between the pastry cases, then spoon in the onion and chorizo mixture.

Bake in a preheated oven, 190°C (375°F), Gas Mark 5, for 20–25 minutes until golden brown and the filling is just set. Leave to cool for 10 minutes, then loosen the edges of the tarts with a knife and remove from the tins. Serve warm or cold with salad.

Spring Onion & Cheddar Tartlets

MAKES 4
PREPARATION TIME 15 minutes
COOKING TIME 25 minutes

1 teaspoon olive oil

2 bunches of large spring onions, trimmed and finely sliced

50 g (2 oz) mature Cheddar, coarsely grated

1 teaspoon chopped thyme

2 eggs, beaten

4 tablespoons low-fat crème fraîche

12 x 15 cm (6 inch) squares of filo pastry

milk, for brushing

Heat the oil in a saucepan, add the spring onions and fry for 1 minute, then remove from heat.

Stir half the Cheddar and the thyme into the spring onion mixture. In a bowl, blend together the remaining Cheddar, the eggs and crème fraîche.

Brush the filo squares with a little milk and use them to line 4 fluted tins, each 10 cm (4 inches) in diameter. Spoon the spring onion mixture into the tins, then pour over the cheese and egg mixture.

Put the tins on a baking sheet and bake in a preheated oven, 200°C (400°F), Gas Mark 6, for 15–20 minutes until the filling is set, then serve.

Stilton &
Leek Tartlets

MAKES 4
PREPARATION TIME 15 minutes
COOKING TIME 25 minutes

1 teaspoon olive oil
8 small leeks, trimmed and
finely sliced
50 g (2 oz) Stilton, crumbled
1 teaspoon chopped thyme
2 eggs, beaten

4 tablespoons low-fat crème
fraîche
12 x 15 cm (6 inch) squares of
filo pastry
milk, for brushing

Heat the oil in a saucepan, add the leeks and fry for
3–4 minutes until softened, then remove from the heat.

Stir half the Stilton and the thyme into the leek mixture.
In a bowl, blend together the remaining Stilton, the eggs
and crème fraîche.

Brush the filo squares with a little milk and use them to
line 4 fluted tins, each 10 cm (4 inches) in diameter. Spoon
the leek mixture into the tins, then pour over the cheese
and egg mixture.

Put the tins on a baking sheet and bake in a preheated
oven, 200°C (400°F), Gas Mark 6, for 15–20 minutes until
the filling is set, then serve.

Pizza Puff Pies

MAKES 6
PREPARATION TIME 25 minutes
COOKING TIME 40 minutes

1 tablespoon olive oil
1 onion, chopped
1 garlic clove, finely chopped
400 g (13 oz) can chopped
   tomatoes
1 teaspoon caster sugar
salt and pepper

500 g (1 lb) ready-made puff
   pastry, defrosted if frozen
flour, for dusting
olive oil, for greasing
small bunch of basil
125 g (4 oz) mozzarella,
   drained
6 pitted black olives (optional)

Heat the oil in a saucepan, add the onion and fry for 5 minutes until softened. Add the garlic, tomatoes and sugar, and season with salt and pepper. Cover and simmer gently for 15 minutes, stirring from time to time until the sauce has thickened. Leave to cool slightly.

Cut the pastry into 6, then roll out each piece on a lightly floured surface and trim to a 15 cm (6 inch) circle using a saucer as a guide. Press each pastry circle into the base of a lightly oiled metal Yorkshire pudding tin or tart tin, 10 cm (4 inches) in diameter, 2.5 cm (1 inch) deep, and press the pastry at intervals to the sides of the tin to give a wavy edge.

Reserve half the smaller basil leaves for garnish, tear the larger leaves into pieces and stir into the sauce. Divide the sauce between the pies and spread into an even layer. Cut the mozzarella into 6 slices and add a slice to each pie. Sprinkle the mozzarella with a little salt and pepper, and add an olive to each, if using.

Bake in a preheated oven, 200°C (400°F), Gas Mark 6, for 20 minutes until the pastry is crisp and golden. Leave to cool for 5 minutes, then turn out. Drizzle with a little olive oil, if liked, sprinkle with remaining basil leaves and serve warm with salad.

Cheesy Chilli Patties

MAKES 4
PREPARATION TIME 30 minutes + chilling
COOKING TIME 30–35 minutes

FOR THE PASTRY

250 g (8 oz) plain flour, plus extra for dusting
1½ teaspoons turmeric
salt
125 g (4 oz) white vegetable fat, diced
2½–3 tablespoons cold water

FOR THE FILLING

2 tablespoons sunflower oil
250 g (8 oz) butternut squash, peeled, halved, deseeded and diced
1 small onion, chopped
2 garlic cloves, finely chopped
½ small hot bonnet chilli, deseeded and finely chopped
1 red or orange pepper, deseeded and diced
100 g (3½ oz) frozen sweetcorn, defrosted
100 g (3½ oz) Red Leicester, diced
2 tablespoons chopped coriander
beaten egg, to glaze
pepper

Make the pastry. Add flour, turmeric, a little salt and the fat to a mixing bowl, and rub the fat in with your fingertips or using an electric mixer until you have fine crumbs. Gradually mix in enough of the measured water to form a soft but not sticky dough. Knead lightly, then wrap in clingfilm and chill while making the filling.

Make the filling. Heat the oil in a frying pan, add the butternut squash and fry for 5 minutes. Add the onion, garlic, chilli and pepper and fry for 5 minutes until the vegetables have softened. Add the sweetcorn, cheese, coriander and a little pepper and cook briefly, then take off the heat and leave to cool.

Cut the pastry into 4 pieces, roll each piece out on a lightly floured surface and trim to an 18 cm (7 inch) circle. Divide the filling between the pastry circles, brush the edges with beaten egg, then fold in half and press the edges together well, first with your fingertips, then with the prongs of a fork, until well sealed.

Transfer to an oiled baking sheet, brush the patties with beaten egg and bake in a preheated oven, 190°C (375°F), Gas Mark 5, for 20–25 minutes. Serve hot or cold with chilli tomato chutney.

Cheesy Picnic Pies

MAKES 4
PREPARATION TIME 25 minutes
COOKING TIME 35 minutes

FOR THE FILLING
1 tablespoon olive oil
1 onion, chopped
2 garlic cloves, finely chopped
1 courgette, diced
½ yellow pepper, deseeded
  and diced
½ red pepper, deseeded
  and diced
400 g (13 oz) can chopped
  tomatoes
1 tablespoon chopped
  rosemary or basil

½ teaspoon caster sugar
beaten egg, to glaze
salt and pepper

FOR THE PASTRY
175 g (6 oz) gluten-free bread
  flour
75 g (3 oz) butter, diced
75 g (3 oz) mature Cheddar,
  diced, plus extra, grated,
  for sprinkling
2 egg yolks
2 teaspoons water

Make the filling. Heat the oil in a saucepan, add the onion and fry for 5 minutes until softened. Add the garlic, courgette and diced peppers and fry briefly, then add the tomatoes, rosemary, sugar and a little salt and pepper. Simmer, uncovered, for 10 minutes, stirring from time to time until thickened. Cool.

Make the pastry. Add the flour, butter and a little salt and pepper to a bowl, rub in the butter until you have fine crumbs, then stir in the cheese. Add the egg yolks and measured water and mix to form a smooth dough.

Knead lightly, then cut the dough into 4 pieces. Roll one of the pieces out between 2 sheets of clingfilm, patting into a neat shape until you have an 18 cm (7 inch) circle. Remove the top sheet of clingfilm, spoon one-quarter of the filling in the centre, brush the pastry edges with beaten egg, then fold the pastry circle in half while still on the lower piece of clingfilm.

Peel the pastry off the film, lift onto an oiled baking sheet, press the edges together well and seal any breaks in the pastry. Repeat with the remaining pastry pieces and filling.

Brush with beaten egg, sprinkle with a little extra cheese and bake in a preheated oven, 190°C (375°F), Gas Mark 5, for 20 minutes until golden brown.

Loosen and transfer to a wire rack. Serve warm or cold with salad.

Devilled Mushroom Pies

MAKES 8
PREPARATION TIME 30 minutes + cooling
COOKING TIME 25 minutes

25 g (1 oz) butter
1 tablespoon olive oil
1 onion, finely chopped
250 g (8 oz) cup mushrooms, sliced
2 garlic cloves, finely chopped
leaves from 3 thyme sprigs, roughly chopped
1 teaspoon Worcestershire sauce
1 teaspoon English mustard

1 teaspoon tomato purée
2 tomatoes, chopped
500 g (1 lb) ready-made puff pastry, defrosted if frozen
flour, for dusting
120 ml (4 fl oz) full-fat crème fraîche
175 g (6 oz) Stilton, diced with rind removed
beaten egg, to glaze
salt and pepper

Heat the butter and oil in a frying pan, add the onion and fry for a few minutes until just beginning to soften. Add the mushrooms and garlic and fry until golden, then add Worcestershire sauce, mustard, tomato purée and tomatoes. Fry for a few minutes until the tomatoes are softened. Take off the heat, add the thyme and leave to cool.

Roll the pastry out thinly on a lightly floured surface and trim to a 35 cm (14 inch) square, then cut into 16 squares. Spoon the mushroom mixture over the centre of 8 of the squares, then top with crème fraîche and cheese. Brush the edges of the pastry with egg, then cover each with a second pastry square.

Press the edges of the pastry together well and crimp the edges, if liked. Transfer to a baking sheet, then slash the tops with a knife, brush with beaten egg and sprinkle with salt flakes and extra thyme, if liked. Bake in a preheated oven, 200°C (400°F), Gas Mark 6, for 20 minutes until well risen and golden brown. Serve warm with salad.

Courgette & Stilton Fritters

MAKES 20
PREPARATION TIME 10 minutes
COOKING TIME 10 minutes

1 tablespoon olive oil
1 large courgette, chopped
3 eggs
150 ml (¼ pint) milk
150 g (5 oz) self-raising flour, sifted

400 g (13 oz) can flageolet beans, drained and rinsed
handful of parsley, chopped
3 spring onions, sliced
325 g (11 oz) can sweetcorn kernels, drained
100 g (3½ oz) Stilton, crumbled

Heat a little of the oil in a nonstick frying pan, add the courgette and fry for 3–4 minutes until golden and tender.

Beat together the eggs, milk and flour in a bowl, then stir in the beans, parsley, spring onions, sweetcorn, Stilton and the cooked courgette.

Heat the remaining oil in a nonstick frying pan and add tablespoons of the mixture to the pan. Gently flatten each fritter and fry for 1–2 minutes on each side until golden. Repeat with the remaining mixture, keeping the fritters warm in a low oven.

When all the fritters are cooked, serve with tomato salsa.

Spinach & Stilton Fritters

MAKES 20
PREPARATION TIME 10 minutes
COOKING TIME 10 minutes

1 tablespoon olive oil
200 g (7 oz) baby spinach
3 eggs
150 ml (¼ pint) milk
150 g (5 oz) self-raising flour, sifted
400 g (13 oz) can cannellini beans, drained and rinsed

handful of parsley, chopped
3 spring onions, sliced
325 g (11 oz) can sweetcorn kernels, drained
100 g (3½ oz) Stilton, crumbled
large pinch of freshly grated nutmeg

Heat a little of the oil in a nonstick frying pan, add the spinach and fry for 1–2 minutes until wilted.

Beat together the eggs, milk and flour in a bowl, then stir in the beans, parsley, spring onions, sweetcorn, Stilton, nutmeg and the cooked spinach.

Heat the remaining oil in a nonstick frying pan and add tablespoons of the mixture to the pan. Gently flatten each fritter and fry for 1–2 minutes on each side until golden. Repeat with the remaining mixture, keeping the fritters warm in a low oven.

When all the fritters are cooked, serve with tomato salsa.

Aubergine Boureks

MAKES 36
PREPARATION TIME 30 minutes
COOKING TIME 15 minutes

2 tablespoons olive oil
1 onion, chopped
1 aubergine, diced
2 garlic cloves, finely chopped
400 g (13 oz) can chopped
   tomatoes
1 teaspoon caster sugar

¼ teaspoon ground allspice
6 sheets filo pastry,
   48 × 23 cm (19 × 9 inches),
   defrosted
100 g (3½ oz) butter, melted
salt and pepper

Heat the oil in a nonstick frying pan, add the onion and aubergine and fry until softened. Add the garlic, tomatoes, sugar, allspice and season with salt and pepper. Cover and simmer for 15–20 minutes until the aubergine is soft. Leave to cool.

Unfold the pastry sheets and put one sheet on the work surface with the long edge facing you. Cover the remaining sheets with clingfilm so that they don't dry out. Brush the pastry in front of you with a little melted butter, then cut into 6 strips, 7.5 × 23 cm (3 × 9 inches). Put a teaspoon of the aubergine mixture near the bottom right corner of each strip.

Holding the bottom right corner of one of the strips, lift and fold up and over diagonally to make a triangular shape to enclose the filling. Fold the bottom left corner straight upwards to make a thicker triangle, then continue folding until you reach the end of the pastry strip.

Make 5 more boureks, then take a second sheet of pastry and repeat. Continue until all the pastry and filling has been used up. Transfer to a baking sheet and brush with the remaining butter. Bake in a preheated oven, 180°C (350°F), Gas Mark 4, for 15 minutes until golden. Leave to cool slightly, then serve warm or cold.

Vegetable Samosas

MAKES 12
PREPARATION TIME 20 minutes
COOKING TIME 15–20 minutes

3 large potatoes, boiled and
  roughly mashed
100 g (3½ oz) cooked peas
1 teaspoon cumin seeds
1 teaspoon amchoor
  (dried mango powder)
2 fresh green chillies,
  deseeded and finely
  chopped
1 small red onion, finely
  chopped

3 tablespoons chopped
  coriander
1 tablespoon chopped mint
  leaves
4 tablespoons lemon juice
12 filo pastry sheets, each
  about 30 x 18 cm
  (12 x 7 inches)
melted butter, for brushing
salt and pepper

In a large bowl, mix together the potatoes, peas, cumin, amchoor, chillies, onion, coriander, mint and lemon juice. Season with salt and pepper to taste and set aside.

Fold each sheet of filo pastry in half lengthways. Put a large spoonful of the potato mixture at one end and then fold the corner of the pastry over the mixture, covering it in a triangular shape. Continue folding over the triangle of pastry along the length of the pastry strip to make a neat triangular samosa.

Place the samosas on a greased baking sheet and brush with melted butter. Bake in a preheated oven at 200°C (400°F), Gas Mark 6, for 15–20 minutes, or until golden.

Serve with mango chutney, if liked.

Baked Curry Puffs

MAKES 8
PREPARATION TIME 20 minutes
COOKING TIME 25 minutes

1 tablespoon sunflower oil
½ small onion, finely chopped
3 garlic cloves, crushed
1 teaspoon grated root ginger
1 red chilli, deseeded and
   finely chopped
2 tablespoons hot curry
   powder
75 g (3 oz) cooked ham,
   chopped

100 g (3½ oz) mashed
   butternut squash
4 tablespoons chopped
   coriander
2 sheets of ready-rolled puff
   pastry, defrosted if frozen
beaten egg, to glaze
salt and pepper

Heat the oil in a wok and add the onion, garlic, ginger and chilli. Stir-fry over a medium heat for 2–3 minutes, then add the curry powder and ham. Stir-fry over a high heat for a further 2–3 minutes, or until the meat is heated through.

Transfer the mixture to a bowl and add the mashed squash and coriander and stir to mix well. Season and set aside.

Use a 7.5 cm (3 inch) cutter to make 8 rounds of puff pastry. Place a large spoonful of the mince mixture onto one half of each round. Brush around the edges of the pastry with the beaten egg, then fold the pastry over to enclose the filling. Using the tines of a fork, press and crimp the edges to seal.

Place the prepared parcels onto a baking sheet lined with nonstick baking paper. Bake in a preheated oven at 220°C (425°F), Gas Mark 7, for 15–20 minutes, or until puffed up and golden in colour. Serve immediately with tomato ketchup, if liked.

Pesto Cigarillos

MAKES 18
PREPARATION TIME 25 minutes
COOKING TIME 10–12 minutes

200 g (7 oz) feta, drained and
    coarsely grated
3 spring onions, very finely
    chopped
3 tablespoons Greek yogurt
1 egg, beaten
3 sheets of filo pastry,
    48 × 23 cm (19 × 9 inches),
    defrosted if frozen

50 g (2 oz) butter, melted
3 tablespoons red pesto
3 tablespoons sesame seeds,
    for sprinkling (optional)
pepper
sea salt flakes

Beat the feta, spring onions, yogurt and egg together and season with a little pepper. Spoon into a piping bag fitted with a large plain nozzle.

Unfold the pastry sheets and put one sheet on your work surface with the long edge facing you. Brush with a little of the melted butter, then spread very thinly with the pesto. Cut into 3 strips, 15 × 23 cm (6 × 9 inches), then cut in half to make 15 × 11 cm (6 × 4½ inch) rectangles.

Pipe a line of the feta cheese mixture about 2.5 cm (1 inch) up from the long side of each rectangle and a little in from the short sides. Fold the short sides in, then the base of the pastry, and roll up to enclose the filling completely and make a thin cigar-type shape. Continue until you have 6 cigarillos from the sheet of pastry.

Repeat with the remaining pastry sheets and feta mixture until both are used up. Arrange on an ungreased baking sheet and brush the outside of each with the remaining butter and sprinkle with a few salt flakes. Bake in a preheated oven, 190°C (375°F), Gas Mark 5, for 10–12 minutes until the pastry is golden brown.

Leave to cool slightly, then serve with salad as a starter or with glasses of chilled white wine as an aperitif.

Pissaldière Bites

MAKES 18
PREPARATION TIME 25 minutes
COOKING TIME 25–30 minutes

2 tablespoons olive oil, plus extra to serve (optional)
250 g (8 oz) onions, thinly sliced
1 garlic clove, finely chopped
1 teaspoon caster sugar
small bunch of thyme

250 g (8 oz) ready-made puff pastry, defrosted if frozen
beaten egg, to glaze
9 anchovy fillets from a can, drained
9 small stuffed green olives
salt and pepper

Heat the oil in a frying pan, add the onions and fry gently for 10 minutes until soft and just beginning to colour. Add the garlic and sugar and fry for a further 5 minutes until golden. Take the pan off the heat, tear leaves from half the thyme over the onion and season with salt and pepper.

Roll the pastry out on a lightly floured surface and trim to a 15 × 30 cm (6 × 12 inch) rectangle, then cut into 5 cm (2 inch) squares. Transfer the squares to an oiled baking sheet, leaving a little space between them.

Brush the tops with beaten egg, then divide the onion mixture between them. Cut each anchovy fillet into 2 thin strips and arrange 2 on each pastry square as a cross, then top with a halved olive.

Bake in a preheated oven, 200°C (400°F), Gas Mark 6, for 10–15 minutes until the pastry is well risen and golden. Brush the olives with a little extra oil, if liked, and sprinkle with the remaining thyme leaves. Serve warm or cold.

Pork Empanadillas

MAKES 8
PREPARATION TIME 15 minutes + cooling
COOKING TIME 35 minutes

3 tablespoons olive oil
250 g (8 oz) minced pork
1 onion, finely chopped
2 garlic cloves, crushed
3 tomatoes, roughly chopped
2 teaspoons tomato purée
1 teaspoon hot smoked
  paprika

1 ready-roasted red pepper
  from a jar, drained and
  chopped
500 g (1 lb) ready-made puff
  pastry, defrosted if frozen
flour, for dusting
beaten egg yolk, to glaze
salt and pepper

Heat half the oil in a frying pan, add the pork, season and fry for 5 minutes, breaking up the clumps, until browned. Remove from the pan and set aside.

Add the remaining oil and the onion to the pan and cook for 5 minutes until softened, then add the garlic and cook for 30 seconds. Add the tomatoes, tomato purée and paprika and cook for a further 5 minutes until pulpy. Return the pork to the pan with the red pepper, stir through and continue to cook for 10–12 minutes, then leave to cool.

Roll out the pastry on a lightly floured work surface until about 5 mm (¼ inch) thick. Using a plate, cut out 8 x 15 cm (6 inch) circles, rerolling the trimmings as necessary. Spoon a little of the pork mixture onto one half of each circle. Brush around the edges with the egg yolk. Fold over the pastry, press out any air and then seal the edges with a fork. Brush with more egg.

Place the pastries on a large baking sheet and bake in a preheated oven, 200°C (400°F), Gas Mark 6, for 15 minutes, or until golden and crisp.

Turkey & Cranberry Turnovers

MAKES 6
PREPARATION TIME 25 minutes
COOKING TIME 20 minutes

1 tablespoon sunflower oil
1 onion, chopped
250 g (8 oz) minced turkey
4 smoked streaky bacon
  rashers, diced
½ teaspoon dried mixed herbs

500 g (1 lb) ready-made puff
  pastry, defrosted if frozen
flour, for dusting
3 tablespoons cranberry
  sauce
beaten egg, to glaze
salt and pepper

Heat the oil in a frying pan, add the onion, turkey and bacon and fry, stirring, for 5 minutes until golden. Take off the heat and stir in the herbs and season with salt and pepper. Leave to cool.

Roll the pastry out thinly on a lightly floured surface and trim to a 25 × 50 cm (10 × 20 inch) rectangle, then cut into 8 × 12 cm (5 inch) squares. Divide the turkey mixture between the squares, top each with a little cranberry sauce, then brush the edges of the pastry with beaten egg.

Fold each pastry square in half to make a triangle, press the edges together well, then slash the tops with criss-cross lines. Transfer to a baking sheet, then brush with beaten egg. Bake in a preheated oven, 200°C (400°F), Gas Mark 6, for 15–20 minutes until well risen and golden. Serve hot or cold.

Turmeric &
Black Pepper Oatcakes

MAKES about 20 small oatcakes
PREPARATION TIME 10–15 minutes
COOKING TIME 20–30 minutes

250 g (8 oz) porridge oats
1 tablespoon olive oil
¼ teaspoon ground turmeric

good pinch of ground black
  pepper
¼ teaspoon sea salt flakes
flour, for dusting

Put the oats into a large bowl. Add the oil, turmeric, pepper and sea salt and mix together.

Half-fill a jug with boiled water and top it up with cool water. Add enough of it to the oats to make them form a ball that binds together. If you add too much water, just add some more oats.

Lightly flour a work surface and roll the ball into a large rectangle about 3 mm (¼ inch) thick. Use a round cutter (about 6–7 cm / 2½–3 inches in diameter) to cut circles, then use a spatula to lift them onto a large baking tray lined with baking paper.

Bake in a preheated oven, 180°C (350°F), Gas Mark 4, for 20–30 minutes, or until golden and crisp. Transfer to a wire rack to cool.

Courgette & Olive Flatbreads

MAKES 2
PREPARATION TIME 20 minutes + rising
COOKING TIME 15–20 minutes

150 g (5 oz) packet pizza
   base mix
flour, for dusting
polenta, for sprinkling
1 small onion, thinly sliced
2 garlic cloves, sliced
2 courgettes, thinly sliced

50 g (2 oz) pitted black olives
4 tablespoons extra virgin
   olive oil, plus extra for
   drizzling
handful of parsley, chopped
salt and pepper

Make the pizza base dough according to the packet instructions. Divide into 2 pieces and roll out each piece on a lightly floured work surface to an oval shape. Scatter a little polenta over 2 baking sheets, then place the bases on the sheets, cover and leave to rise for 15 minutes.

Place the onion, garlic, courgettes, olives and oil in a bowl and gently toss together, then season well.

Scatter the mixture over the bases and drizzle over a little extra oil. Bake in a preheated oven, 200°C (400°F), Gas Mark 6, for 15–20 minutes until crisp. Scatter over the parsley and serve.

Fragrant Naan

MAKES 8
PREPARATION TIME 20 minutes + resting
COOKING TIME about 20 minutes

450 g (14½ oz) self-raising flour,
plus extra for dusting
2 teaspoons sugar
1 teaspoon salt
1 teaspoon baking powder
4 tablespoons melted butter
or ghee, plus extra for
brushing

250 ml (8 fl oz) warm milk
1 garlic clove, finely chopped
4 tablespoons coriander,
roughly chopped

Sift the flour, sugar, salt and baking powder in a large mixing bowl. Add the melted butter or ghee and rub into the flour mixture with your fingers. Gradually add the warm milk and mix to a soft dough.

Transfer to a lightly floured surface and knead for 6–8 minutes, or until smooth. Place in the bowl, cover with clingfilm and set aside for 20–25 minutes.

Divide the mixture into 8 portions and flatten each one into a thick cake. Cover with a cloth and set aside for 10–15 minutes.

Roll each piece into a disc about 23 cm (9 inches) in diameter. Brush the tops of the breads with butter or ghee and sprinkle over the garlic and coriander.

Place the breads on a lightly oiled grill rack and cook in batches under a preheated medium–high grill for 1–2 minutes on each side, or until puffed up and lightly browned in spots. Wrap in a clean tea towel while you finish cooking the rest.

Serve warm with a curry of your choice.

Ham & Cheese Scones

MAKES 8
PREPARATION TIME 15 minutes + cooling
COOKING TIME 12 minutes

175 g (6 oz) rice flour, plus extra for dusting
75 g (3 oz) potato flour
1 teaspoon xanthan gum
1 teaspoon baking powder
1 teaspoon bicarbonate of soda
75 g (3 oz) butter, cubed

25 g (1 oz) honey-roast ham, roughly chopped
2 tablespoons grated Parmesan
1 tablespoon chopped parsley
1 large egg, beaten
4 tablespoons buttermilk, plus extra for brushing

Place the flours, xanthan gum, baking powder, bicarbonate of soda and butter in a food processor and whiz until the mixture resembles fine breadcrumbs, or rub in by hand in a large bowl.

Stir the ham, Parmesan and parsley into the mixture, then, using the blade of a knife, stir in the egg and buttermilk until the mixture comes together.

Tip the dough out onto a lightly floured surface and gently press it down to a thickness of 2.5 cm (1 inch). Use a 5 cm (2 inch) cutter to cut out the scones.

Place on a lightly floured baking sheet and brush with a little buttermilk. Bake in a preheated oven, 220°C (425°F), Gas Mark 7, for about 12 minutes until golden and risen. Remove the scones from the oven and transfer to a wire rack to cool.

Rosemary, Bacon & Brie Muffins

MAKES 8
PREPARATION TIME 20 minutes
COOKING TIME 25 minutes

75 g (3 oz) rindless streaky
   bacon rashers, finely
   chopped
225 g (7½ oz) plain flour
1½ teaspoons baking powder
1 teaspoon bicarbonate
   of soda
1 teaspoon sweet paprika
2 large eggs

¼ teaspoon black pepper
pinch of salt
2 teaspoons finely chopped
   rosemary
150 ml (¼ pint) milk
75 g (3 oz) butter, melted, plus
   extra for greasing
125 g (4 oz) firm Brie, cut
   into cubes

Cook the bacon in a large frying pan over a medium–high heat for 4–5 minutes, stirring occasionally, until golden. Drain on kitchen paper.

Meanwhile, sift the flour into a large bowl with the baking powder, bicarbonate of soda and paprika.

Break the eggs into a jug and beat lightly. Add the pepper, salt, rosemary, milk and melted butter and whisk together. Pour the mixture into the dry ingredients, then add two-thirds of both the Brie and cooked bacon and stir until just barely combined.

Grease a 12-cup muffin tin. Divide the mixture between the holes and then top with the remaining bacon and Brie. Bake in a preheated oven, 200 °C (400 °F), Gas Mark 6, for 20 minutes until risen and golden. Serve warm.

The
Classics

Stilton
Soufflés

MAKES 2
PREPARATION TIME 10 minutes
COOKING TIME 15 minutes

15 g (½ oz) butter, plus extra
   for greasing
1 tablespoon grated
   Parmesan

15 g (½ oz) plain flour
100 ml (3½ oz) milk
50 g (1¾ oz) Stilton, crumbled
1 egg, separated

Butter 2 ramekins, each holding 150 ml (¼ pint), and coat
the bottom and sides with grated Parmesan.

Melt the butter in a small saucepan and add the flour.
Whisk to make a smooth paste, then gradually add the
milk, stirring all the time, until the sauce thickens. Remove
from the heat, allow to cool a little, then beat in the Stilton
and egg yolk.

Whisk the egg white in a clean bowl until it forms soft
peaks. Fold into the cheese mixture, and then spoon into
the prepared ramekins. Bake in a preheated oven, 200°C
(400°F), Gas Mark 6, for 15 minutes, or until golden and
risen. Serve immediately with a watercress salad and some
crusty, seeded bread.

Goats' Cheese & Herb Soufflés

MAKES 4
PREPARATION TIME 10 minutes
COOKING TIME 15 minutes

25 g (1 oz) butter, plus extra
   for greasing
50 g (2 oz) plain flour
300 ml (½ pint) milk
4 eggs, separated
100 g (3½ oz) soft goats'
   cheese, crumbled

1 tablespoon chopped
   mixed herbs
1 tablespoon grated
   Parmesan
salt and pepper

Melt the butter in a saucepan, add the flour and cook, stirring, for 1 minute. Gradually whisk in the milk, and cook for 2 minutes until thickened.

Remove the pan from the heat. Beat in the egg yolks one at a time, then stir in the goats' cheese. Season well.

Whisk the egg whites in a large bowl until they form soft peaks, then gradually fold them into the cheese mixture with the herbs. Transfer to four greased (150 ml / ¼ pint) ramekins and sprinkle over the Parmesan. Bake in a preheated oven, 190°C (375°F), Gas Mark 5, for 10–12 minutes until risen and golden.

Serve with a rocket salad.

Gruyère &
Mustard Soufflés

MAKES 4
PREPARATION TIME 10 minutes
COOKING TIME 15 minutes

25 g (1 oz) butter, plus extra for
    greasing
50 g (2 oz) plain flour
2 teaspoons English
    mustard powder
300 ml (½ pint) milk

4 eggs, separated
75 g (3 oz) Gruyère, grated
1 tablespoon chopped
    mixed herbs
salt and pepper

Melt the butter in a saucepan, add the flour and mustard
and cook, stirring, for 1 minute. Gradually whisk in milk,
and cook for 2 minutes until thickened.

Remove the pan from the heat. Beat in the egg yolks
one at a time, then stir in the cheese. Season well.

Whisk the egg whites in a large bowl until they form soft
peaks, then gradually fold them into the cheese mixture
with the herbs. Transfer to four greased (150 ml / ¼ pint)
ramekins. Bake in a preheated oven, 190°C (375°F), Gas
Mark 5, for 10–12 minutes until risen and golden.

Serve with a rocket salad

Beetroot Tarte Tatin

SERVES 6
PREPARATION TIME 5 minutes
COOKING TIME 45 minutes + standing

320 g (11 oz) vegan puff pastry, defrost if frozen
2 tablespoons olive oil
2 red onions, finely sliced
1 tablespoon caster sugar
1 tablespoon balsamic vinegar

leaves from 2 thyme sprigs, plus extra to serve
400 g (13 oz) cooked beetroot, cut into wedges
salt and pepper

Roll out the pastry to 5 mm (¼ inch) thick. Use a dinner plate as large as the ovenproof frying pan in which you will cook the tarte, as a template to cut out a circle of pastry and place on a sheet of nonstick baking paper. Transfer this to a tray and keep in the refrigerator until needed.

Heat the oil in the ovenproof frying pan and fry the onions for 15 minutes over a low heat or until soft and deeply caramelized.

Sprinkle over the sugar, vinegar and thyme and stir well to combine. Add the beetroot wedges in a snug single layer in a concentric circle pattern. Turn off the heat.

Cover the onions and beetroots with the puff pastry circle, tucking the edges down the side of the pan.

Bake in a preheated oven, 200°C (400°F), Gas Mark 6, for 30 minutes until the pastry is golden and well risen. Remove from the oven and leave to stand for 10 minutes before inverting onto a large serving dish. Scatter with thyme leaves and season well with salt and pepper.

French Onion Tarts

MAKES 12

PREPARATION TIME 30 minutes + chilling

COOKING TIME 30–35 minutes

1 quantity all-butter
   shortcrust pastry
   (see page 7)
flour, for dusting
50 g (2 oz) butter
2 onions, thinly sliced

4 eggs
200 ml (7 fl oz) milk
2 teaspoons Dijon mustard
125 g (4 oz) Gruyère, finely
   grated
salt and pepper

Roll the pastry out thinly on a lightly floured surface, then stamp out 12 x 10 cm (4 inch) circles, with a plain cutter, and press into the greased holes of a 12-cup muffin tin. Reroll the pastry trimmings as needed. Chill for 15 minutes.

Heat the butter in a frying pan, add the onions and fry over a gentle heat for 10 minutes, stirring from time to time until softened and just beginning to colour.

Add the eggs, milk and mustard to a large wide-necked jug, and fork together until just mixed. Add the cheese and seasoning, and mix together. Divide the mixture between the pastry cases, then spoon in the fried onions.

Bake in a preheated oven, 190°C (375°F), Gas Mark 5, for 20–25 minutes until golden brown and the filling is just set. Leave to cool for 10 minutes, then loosen the edges of the tarts with a knife and remove from the tins.

Serve warm or cold with salad.

Trout &
Asparagus Tarts

MAKES 4
PREPARATION TIME 10 minutes + chilling
COOKING TIME 25 minutes

FOR THE PASTRY
200 g (7 oz) plain flour
100 g (3½ oz) chilled butter,
 diced
about 100 ml (3½ fl oz) cold
 water

FOR THE FILLING
8 asparagus spears, trimmed
 and halved
75 g (3 oz) smoked trout,
 flaked
150 ml (¼ pint) crème fraîche
1 egg, beaten
50 g (2 oz) feta, crumbled
black pepper

Make the pastry. Sift the flour into a large bowl, add the butter and rub in with your fingertips until the mixture resembles fine breadcrumbs. Add enough cold water to make a ball. Bring the dough together, wrap in clingfilm and chill for 30 minutes.

Divide the pastry into 4, roll out each piece and use it to line 4 lightly greased tartlet tins, each 9 cm (3½ inches) across. Bake blind (bake the empty cases without filling) in a preheated oven, 200°C (400°F), Gas Mark 6, for 5 minutes. Then remove the tins from the oven, but leave the oven on.

Make the filling. Simmer the asparagus in boiling water for 1 minute, then drain. Arrange the asparagus in the pastry cases (still in their tins) with the smoked trout. Whisk the crème fraîche and egg together and season well with black pepper. Stir through the feta.

Pour the mixture into the pastry cases (still in their tartlet tins) and bake for 15–20 minutes, or until golden and puffy.

Serve with a side salad.

Spinach
& Feta Tarts

MAKES 4
PREPARATION TIME 10 minutes + chilling
COOKING TIME 25 minutes

FOR THE PASTRY
200 g (7 oz) plain flour
100 g (3½ oz) chilled butter,
  diced
about 100 ml (3½ fl oz) cold
  water

FOR THE FILLING
150 g (5 oz) baby leaf spinach
150 ml (¼ pint) crème fraîche
1 egg, beaten
50 g (2 oz) feta, crumbled
grated nutmeg
black pepper

Make the pastry. Sift the flour into a large bowl, add the butter and rub in with your fingertips until the mixture resembles fine breadcrumbs. Add enough cold water to make a ball. Bring the dough together, wrap in clingfilm and chill for 30 minutes.

Divide the pastry into 4, roll out each piece and use it to line 4 lightly greased tartlet tins, each 9 cm (3½ inches) across. Bake blind (bake the empty cases without filling) in a preheated oven, 200°C (400°F), Gas Mark 6, for 5 minutes. Then remove the cases, but leave the oven on.

Make the filling. Put the spinach in a large colander, pour over boiling water to wilt the leaves, then squeeze out any liquid. Divide the spinach among the pastry cases. Whisk together the crème fraîche and egg and season well with grated nutmeg and black pepper. Stir through the feta. Pour the mixture into the pastry cases (still in their tartlet tins) and cook for 15–20 minutes, or until golden and puffy. Serve with a side salad.

Brie, Thyme & Onion Tart

MAKES 4
PREPARATION TIME 10 minutes
COOKING TIME 20 minutes

375 g (12 oz) ready-rolled
shortcrust pastry
butter, for greasing
25 g (4 oz) onion chutney

200 g (7 oz) Brie or
Camembert, sliced
1 teaspoon dried thyme
4 teaspoons chilli oil, garlic oil
or basil oil

Roll out the shortcrust pastry on a large greased baking sheet and fold in the edges by about 1 cm (½ inch) to create a crust.

Spread the onion chutney onto the pastry, then top with the cheese. Scatter over the thyme and drizzle with the oil.

Bake in a preheated oven, 200°C (400°F), Gas Mark 6, for about 20 minutes until the pastry is crisp and golden and the cheese has melted.

Serve with a tomato salad.

Cheese, Tomato & Basil Muffins

MAKES 8
PREPARATION TIME 10 minutes
COOKING TIME 20–25 minutes

spray oil, for oiling
150 g (5 oz) self-raising flour
½ teaspoon salt
100 g (3½ oz) fine cornmeal
65 g (2½ oz) Cheddar, grated
50 g (2 oz) sun-dried tomatoes
    in oil, drained and chopped

2 tablespoons chopped basil
1 egg
300 ml (½ pint) milk
2 tablespoons extra virgin
    olive oil
butter, to serve

Lightly oil 8 muffin tin holes with spray oil. Sift the flour and salt into a bowl and stir in the cornmeal, 50 g (2 oz) of the cheese, the tomatoes and basil. Make a well in the centre.

Beat the egg, milk and oil together in a separate bowl or jug, pour into the well and stir together until just combined. The batter should remain a little lumpy.

Divide the batter between the prepared muffin holes and scatter over the remaining cheese. Bake in a preheated oven, 180°C (350°F), Gas Mark 4, for 20–25 minutes until risen and golden. Leave to cool in the tin for 5 minutes, then transfer to a wire rack to cool. Serve warm with butter.

Cheesy Herby Muffins

MAKES 8
PREPARATION TIME 5 minutes
COOKING TIME 20 minutes

175 g (6 oz) Gruyère, grated
3 spring onions, finely sliced
1 teaspoon thyme leaves
1 tablespoon chopped parsley
100 g (3½ oz) rice flour
½ teaspoon baking powder
150 g (5 oz) fresh breadcrumbs
1 teaspoon English mustard
3 eggs, beaten
50 g (2 oz) butter, melted
4 tablespoons milk

Line a muffin tray with 8 paper cases.

Mix together all the ingredients in a large bowl until just combined and spoon the mixture into the cases.

Bake in a preheated oven, 190°C (170°F), Gas Mark 5, for 20 minutes, or until golden and just firm to the touch. Remove from the oven and serve warm.

Caramelized Onion & Feta Muffins

MAKES 8
PREPARATION TIME 5 minutes
COOKING TIME 33 minutes

1 tablespoon olive oil
1 onion, thinly sliced
1 teaspoon caster sugar
100 g (3½ oz) feta, crumbled
1 tablespoon chopped thyme
100 g (3½ oz) rice flour

½ teaspoon baking powder
150 g (5 oz) fresh breadcrumbs
1 teaspoon English mustard
3 eggs, beaten
50 g (2 oz) butter, melted
4 tablespoons milk

Heat the oil in a saucepan, add the onion and fry over a low heat for about 10 minutes until very soft and beginning to brown. Add the sugar and continue to cook for 2–3 minutes.

Line a muffin tray with 8 paper cases.

Mix together the remaining ingredients in a large bowl until just combined and then spoon the mixture into the muffin cases.

Bake in a preheated oven, 200°C (400°F), Gas Mark 6, for 20 minutes until golden and firm to the touch. Remove from the oven and serve warm.

Sausage Rolls

MAKES 15
PREPARATION TIME 15 minutes + chilling
COOKING TIME 15 minutes

400 g (13 oz) good-quality
    sausages
200 g (7 oz) plain flour, plus
    extra for dusting
50 g (2 oz) wholemeal flour
pinch of salt

150 g (5 oz) butter, chilled
    and diced
3 tablespoons iced water
1 tablespoon poppy seeds
beaten egg, to glaze

Snip each sausage at one end and squeeze the sausage meat out onto a chopping board lightly dusted with flour. Roll out into thinner sausages.

Sift both flours and the salt into a bowl. Add the butter and rub it in with your fingertips until the mixture resembles fine breadcrumbs. Add enough of the measured iced water to mix to a soft dough, then stir in the poppy seeds. Turn the dough out onto a lightly floured surface and knead briefly.

Roll the pastry out on a well-floured surface to a rectangle measuring 30 x 25 cm (12 x 10 inches), then cut into three 10 x 25 cm (4 x 10 inch) strips. Lay the sausage meat down the centre of each strip. Brush 1 edge of each strip with beaten egg, roll over and flute the edges. Cut each strip into five 5 cm (2 inch) sausage rolls and put on a baking sheet.

Make a couple of cuts in the top of each roll and brush with the remaining egg. Refrigerate for 15 minutes before baking in a preheated oven, 200°C (400°F), Gas Mark 6, for 15 minutes. Remove from the oven and leave to cool before lifting off the sheet.

Olive & Sun-Blush Tomato Swirls

MAKES 12
PREPARATION TIME 15 minutes + proving & cooling
COOKING TIME 20 minutes

500 g (1 lb) strong plain flour, plus extra for sifting
7 g (¼ oz) sachet fast-action dried yeast
pinch of salt
2 tablespoons olive oil
300 ml (½ pint) warm water

1 onion, thinly sliced
100 g (3½ oz) pitted olives, roughly chopped
75 g (3 oz) sun-blush tomatoes
½ teaspoon fennel seeds
2 tablespoons chopped parsley

Place the flour, yeast and salt in a large bowl. Combine half the oil with the measured water and stir into the flour to form a dough.

Turn the dough out on a lightly floured surface and knead for 5 minutes until smooth and elastic. Place in a lightly oiled bowl, cover with a damp cloth and set aside in a warm place for about 1 hour until doubled in size.

Meanwhile, heat the remaining oil in a frying pan, add the onion and fry for 7–8 minutes until softened and golden, then stir in the olives, tomatoes and fennel seeds. Leave to cool.

Roll the dough out on a floured surface to the size of an A4 sheet of paper and spread with the onion mixture. Roll up the dough from one long end and cut the roll into 12 rounds. Lay the rounds on a large baking sheet dusted with flour, cover with a damp cloth and leave to rise for 30 minutes.

Bake in a preheated oven, 220°C (425°F), Gas Mark 7, for 12–15 minutes until golden. Transfer to a wire rack to cool.

Mains

Tuscan-Style Tarts

MAKES 4
PREPARATION TIME 10 minutes
COOKING TIME 15 minutes

375 g (12 oz) ready-rolled puff
pastry, defrosted if frozen
2 tomatoes, sliced
150 g (5 oz) ready-cooked
chicken, sliced
8 small pieces of ready-
roasted red pepper, from
a jar, drained

1 tablespoon thyme leaves
125 g (4 oz) Kalamata olives
1 tablespoon olive oil
salt and pepper

Unroll the ready-rolled puff pastry, cut it into 4 x 12 cm
(5 inch) circles and place, well spaced apart, on a large
baking sheet. Prick the bases all over with a fork.

Arrange the tomato slices randomly on top of each one,
dividing them evenly between the bases and keeping a
1 cm (½ inch) border around the edge. Evenly scatter over
the chicken, peppers, thyme and olives, then drizzle with
the olive oil and season to taste.

Bake at the top of a preheated oven, 220°C (425°F),
Gas Mark 7, for 12–15 minutes, or until the pastry is puffed
and golden and the topping soft. Serve the tarts with a
simple green salad.

Caramelized Onion & Anchovy Tart

MAKES 4
PREPARATION TIME 25 minutes + chilling
COOKING TIME 55 minutes–1 hour

FOR THE PASTRY
200 g (7 oz) plain flour, plus extra for dusting
85 g (3¼ oz) chilled lightly salted butter, cubed
1 egg
1 egg yolk

FOR THE FILLING
25 g (1 oz) butter
2 tablespoons olive oil
3 large onions, finely sliced
2 thyme sprigs
2 eggs
100 ml (3½ fl oz) milk
100 ml (3½ fl oz) double cream
2 tomatoes, thinly sliced
8 anchovy fillets from a can, drained
salt and pepper

Make the pastry. Place all the pastry ingredients in a food processor and blend until they form a soft dough, adding a drop of cold water if necessary.

Knead lightly until smooth, then wrap in clingfilm and chill for at least 30 minutes.

Roll out the pastry on a lightly floured work surface until about 3 mm (⅛ inch) thick and use to line a 23 cm (9 inch) fluted tart tin. Trim off the excess pastry and chill for 1 hour.

Line the tart with baking paper and fill with baking beans. Bake in a preheated oven, 180°C (350°F), Gas Mark 4, for 10–12 minutes until lightly golden. Remove the baking paper and beans, then return to the oven and cook for a further 2 minutes to dry out the base. Remove from the oven and leave to cool, leaving the oven on.

Make the filling. Heat the butter and oil in a frying pan, add the onions and thyme and fry over a low heat for about 20 minutes until the onions are golden brown.

Remove the thyme and spread the onions over the tart base. Whisk together the eggs, milk and cream in a bowl, season with salt and pepper and pour over the onions.

Bake in the oven for 10 minutes until slightly risen and starting to set. Arrange the tomatoes and anchovies on top of the tart, then return to the oven and cook for a further 10–15 minutes until the filling has set completely. Leave to cool for 5 minutes before serving.

Potato & Onion Pizza

SERVES 4
PREPARATION TIME 15 minutes
COOKING TIME 30 minutes

300 g (10 oz) plain flour
7 g (¼ oz) sachet fast-action
  dried yeast
1½ teaspoons caster sugar
1 teaspoon salt
175 ml (6 fl oz) warm water
3 tablespoons olive oil, plus
  extra for oiling
125 ml (4 fl oz) crème fraîche

200 g (7 oz) unpeeled new
  potatoes, very thinly sliced
  on a mandolin
½ onion, very thinly sliced on
  a mandolin
2 teaspoons dried thyme
100 g (3½ oz) Emmental
  or Cheddar, grated
12 black olives (optional)
cracked black pepper

Mix the flour, yeast, sugar and salt together in a large bowl. Make a well in the centre and pour in the measured water and 2 tablespoons of the oil. Combine to make a soft dough, then roll out to a rectangle about 35 x 25 cm (14 x 10 inches). Transfer to a lightly oiled baking sheet. Bake in a preheated oven, 200°C (400°F), Gas Mark 6, for 5 minutes, or until just beginning to colour.

Spoon 4 tablespoons of the crème fraîche over the pizza base. Top with the slices of potato and onion, then sprinkle over the thyme and scatter with the cheese.

Drizzle the remaining oil over the pizza and return to the oven. Increase the temperature to 220°C (425°F), Gas Mark 7, and bake for about 15 minutes until golden.

Cut the pizza into slices, scatter with the olives, if using, and top with the remaining crème fraîche. Season with cracked black pepper and serve hot.

Cockle, Leek & Bacon Pies

MAKES 6
PREPARATION TIME 45 minutes + chilling
COOKING TIME 50–55 minutes

FOR THE FILLING
600 ml (1 pint) milk
200 g (7 oz) leeks, trimmed,
    thinly sliced, white and
    green parts kept separate
2 bay leaves
250 g (8 oz) gammon steak
50 g (2 oz) butter
50 g (2 oz) plain flour
200 g (7 oz) cockles, defrosted
    if frozen

beaten egg, to glaze
salt and pepper

FOR THE PASTRY
375 g (12 oz) plain flour
175 g (6 oz) mixed butter and
    white vegetable fat, diced
4–4½ tablespoons cold water
salt and pepper

Make the filling. Pour the milk into a saucepan, add the white sliced leeks, bay leaves and salt and pepper, then bring to the boil. Set aside for 10 minutes. Grill the gammon steak on a foil-lined grill pan for 7–8 minutes, turning once, until cooked. Trim off the fat, then dice the meat.

Heat the butter in a saucepan, stir in the flour, cook for 1–2 minutes, then gradually mix in the strained milk.

Bring to the boil, stirring until smooth. Discard the bay leaves, then return the white leeks to the sauce, add the green sliced leeks and cook gently for 2–3 minutes, stirring until the leeks are just cooked. Leave to cool.

Make the pastry according to the method on page 7. Wrap the dough in clingfilm and chill for 15 minutes.

Reserve one-third of the pastry, roll out the remainder thinly, then cut six 15 cm (6 inch) circles. Press into buttered individual tart tins, 10 cm (4 inches) in diameter and 2.5 cm (1 inch) deep. Trim off the excess pastry and reroll the trimmings as needed.

Stir the cockles and gammon into the sauce, then spoon into the pastry bases. Brush the edges with egg. Roll out the reserved pastry and cut 12 cm (5 inch) circles for the lids. Press the pastry edges together and flute (see page 9), prick the top to let steam escape, then brush with beaten egg. Decorate (see page 9) and sprinkle with salt and pepper.

Bake the pies on a baking sheet in a preheated oven, 190°C (375°F), Gas Mark 5, for 30–35 minutes until golden brown. Serve with steamed baby carrots.

Wild Mushroom & Beetroot Wellington

SERVES 4–6
PREPARATION TIME 20 minutes + soaking
COOKING TIME 1 hour

2 tablespoons olive oil

2 shallots, roughly chopped

2 garlic cloves, roughly chopped

15 g (½ oz) dried wild mushrooms, soaked in boiling water for 30 minutes, drained and chopped

300 g (10 oz) chestnut mushrooms, roughly chopped

200 g (7 oz) green lentils, drained and rinsed

½ tablespoon light soy sauce

½ tablespoon vegan red wine vinegar

1 tablespoon thyme leaves

1 tablespoon parsley leaves, roughly chopped

25 g (1 oz) stale breadcrumbs

75 g (3 oz) ready-cooked, peeled chestnuts, roughly chopped

320 g (11 oz) sheet of ready-rolled vegan puff pastry, defrost if frozen

100 g (3½ oz) spinach

25 ml (1 fl oz) oat milk, to glaze

30 g (1 oz) black or white sesame seeds, or a mixture

salt and pepper

onion gravy (optional)

Heat the olive oil in a large, shallow ovenproof frying pan or casserole dish (preferably 30 cm / 12 inches diameter) and fry the shallots and garlic over a medium heat. Cook for about 5 minutes until soft.

Add all the mushrooms into the shallot mixture and cook until soft.

Add the lentils, soy sauce, vinegar and herbs. Season with salt and pepper to taste. Cook the mixture for a further 5 minutes to allow the flavours to meld before turning off the heat and mixing in the breadcrumbs and the ready-cooked chestnuts. Once fully combined, scoop the mixture into a separate bowl and allow to cool.

Wilt the spinach with boiling hot water poured over in a sieve. Squeeze out the excess water and set aside.

Wipe the pan clean. Roll out the pastry sheet into the pan (keeping it on its paper) and spread the spinach evenly in the middle, leaving a border of pastry around the edge.

Transfer the mushroom mixture from the bowl onto the spinach and roughly form a big sausage shape. Fold in the shorter sides, then fold up the pastry margin over the filling and continue rolling up the pastry, tucking in the sides as you go, rather like a large spring roll or burrito, to encase the filling. Position the roll with the seal on the underside.

Score the top of the roll in a decorative pattern with a sharp knife, brush the pastry with oat milk and scatter over the sesame seeds. Bake in a preheated oven, 200°C (400°F), Gas Mark 6, for 55 minutes until the pastry is golden brown.

Slice up and serve with onion gravy, if preferred.

Chicken Bisteeya

SERVES 6
PREPARATION TIME 40 minutes
COOKING TIME 1 hour 50 minutes

4 chicken thigh and
  drumstick joints
1 onion, chopped
1 cinnamon stick, halved
2.5 cm (1 inch) root ginger,
  finely chopped
¼ teaspoon turmeric
600 ml (1 pint) water
3 tablespoons chopped
  coriander
3 tablespoons chopped
  parsley
40 g (1½ oz) raisins

40 g (1½ oz) blanched
  almonds, roughly chopped
4 eggs
200 g (7 oz) chilled filo pastry
65 g (2½ oz) butter, melted
salt and pepper

TO GARNISH
icing sugar, sifted
ground cinnamon

Pack the chicken into a large saucepan and scatter over the onion, then add the cinnamon, ginger, turmeric and salt and pepper. Cover the chicken with the measured water. Cover and simmer for 1 hour until tender. Lift the chicken out of the stock and transfer to a plate to cool.

Boil the stock rapidly for about 10 minutes until reduced by one-third.

Dice the chicken, discarding the skin and bones. Strain the stock into a jug. Discard the cinnamon stick, then add the herbs, raisins and almonds to the chicken. Whisk 200 ml (7 fl oz) of the stock into the eggs.

Brush a 23 cm (9 inch) springform tin with a little of the melted butter. Unfold the pastry, then place one of the sheets in the tin so that it half covers the base and drapes up over the side and hangs over the top of the tin. Add a second pastry sheet overlapping a little over the first and brush with a little melted butter. Continue adding pastry, brushing alternate sheets with melted butter until two-thirds of the pastry has been used and the tin is thickly covered.

Spoon in the chicken mixture, then cover with the eggs and stock. Arrange the remaining pastry over the top in a smooth layer, then fold in the sides in soft pleats, brushing layers of pastry with butter as you go. Brush the top layer with the remaining butter.

Bake in a preheated oven, 180°C (350°F), Gas Mark 4, for 40–45 minutes until golden brown and the filling is set.

Leave to cool for 15 minutes, then remove from the tin. Dust with icing sugar and cinnamon and serve warm.

Cheesy Tuna & Chive Pasties

MAKES 4
PREPARATION TIME 15 minutes
COOKING TIME 20 minutes

50 g (2 oz) butter
2 leeks, finely sliced
500 g (1 lb) ready-made puff
    pastry, defrost if frozen
flour, for dusting
2 x 185 g (6½ oz) cans tuna in
    olive oil, drained

175 g (6 oz) cold mashed
    potato
100 g (3½ oz) mature Cheddar,
    grated
1½ tablespoons chopped
    chives
beaten egg, to glaze
salt and pepper

Melt the butter in a large frying pan and cook the leeks for 4–5 minutes until softened.

Meanwhile, roll out the pastry on a lightly floured work surface and stamp out four 22 cm (8½ inch) circles.

Transfer the leeks to a large bowl, add the tuna, potato, cheese, chives and a pinch of salt and pepper and mix well.

Spoon the mixture into the middle of each pastry circle, then brush a little beaten egg around the border. Fold up the pastry, pinching and crimping the edges together along the top to encase the filling.

Arrange the pasties on a baking sheet lined with baking paper and brush with beaten egg. Bake in a preheated oven, 220°C (425°F), Gas Mark 7, for about 15 minutes, or until puffed and golden. Cool slightly and serve with salad leaves.

Chillied Beef Parcels

MAKES 6
PREPARATION TIME 30 minutes
COOKING TIME 1 hour 10 minutes

FOR THE FILLING
2 teaspoons sunflower oil
250 g (8 oz) minced beef
1 small onion, chopped
1 garlic clove, finely chopped
½ teaspoon dried crushed
  chillies
¼ teaspoon ground cinnamon
2 teaspoons light muscovado
  sugar
1 bay leaf
200 g (7 oz) can chopped
  tomatoes

200 g (7 oz) can red kidney
  beans, drained and rinsed
150 ml (¼ pint) beef stock
beaten egg, to glaze
salt and pepper

FOR THE PASTRY
300 g (10 oz) plain flour, plus
  extra for dusting
50 g (2 oz) polenta
75 g (3 oz) butter, diced
75 g (3 oz) white vegetable fat,
  diced
4–4½ tablespoons cold water

Make the filling. Heat the oil in a saucepan, add the mince and onion and fry, stirring, until the mince is browned. Stir in the garlic, chillies, cinnamon, sugar and bay leaf. Mix in the tomatoes, kidney beans and stock, then add plenty of salt and pepper. Bring to the boil, stirring, then cover and simmer gently for 45 minutes. Leave to cool.

Make the pastry. Add the flour, polenta, fats and a little salt and pepper to a bowl. Rub in the fats with your fingertips or use an electric mixer until you have fine crumbs. Add enough water to form a smooth dough, then knead lightly on a surface dusted with flour.

Cut the pastry in half, roll out one half and trim to a 12 × 38 cm (5 × 15 inch) rectangle, then cut into three 12 cm (5 inch) squares. Spoon half the filling into the centre of the pastry squares. Brush the edges with beaten egg, then bring the points of the pastry up to the centre, pressing the straight edges of the pastry together.

Transfer to an oiled baking sheet and repeat with the remaining pastry and filling to make 6 pies. Brush the pies with beaten egg. Bake in a preheated oven, 190°C (375°F), Gas Mark 5, for 20 minutes.

Serve hot with soured cream and chunky salsa.

Creamy Mushroom & Stilton Pies

MAKES 8
PREPARATION TIME 30 minutes + cooling
COOKING TIME 25 minutes

25 g (1 oz) butter
1 tablespoon olive oil
1 onion, finely chopped
250 g (8 oz) mixed mushrooms, finely sliced
2 garlic cloves, finely chopped
3 sprigs thyme, leaves torn from stems, plus extra to decorate

500 g (1 lb) ready-made puff pastry, defrosted if frozen
flour, for dusting
120 ml (4 fl oz) full-fat crème fraîche
175 g (6 oz) Stilton, diced with rind removed
beaten egg, to glaze
salt and pepper

Heat the butter and oil in a frying pan, add the onion and fry for a few minutes until just beginning to soften, then add the mushrooms and garlic and fry, stirring until golden. Take off the heat, add the thyme leaves and leave to cool.

Roll the pastry out thinly on a lightly floured surface and trim to a 35 cm (14 inch) square, then cut into 16 squares. Spoon the mushroom mixture over the centre of 8 of the squares, then top with crème fraîche and cheese. Brush the edges of the pastry with egg, then cover each with a second pastry square.

Press the edges of the pastry together well and crimp the edges, if liked. Transfer to a baking sheet, then slit the tops with a knife, brush with beaten egg and sprinkle with salt flakes and extra thyme, if liked. Bake in a preheated oven, 200°C (400°F), Gas Mark 6, for 20 minutes until well risen and golden brown. Serve warm with salad.

Chicken & Mushroom Pies

MAKES 4
PREPARATION TIME 35 minutes + chilling
COOKING TIME 1 hour 10 minutes

FOR THE FILLING
1 tablespoon olive oil
8 boneless, skinless chicken thighs, about 625 g (1¼ lb), cubed
1 onion, chopped
2 garlic cloves, finely chopped
2 tablespoons plain flour
150 ml (¼ pint) white wine
200 ml (7 fl oz) chicken stock
a few sprigs thyme or a little dried thyme
25 g (1 oz) butter

125 g (4 oz) closed-cup mushrooms, sliced
beaten egg, to glaze
salt and pepper

FOR THE PASTRY
300 g (10 oz) plain flour
1½ teaspoons mustard powder
150 g (5 oz) mixed butter and white vegetable fat, diced
3 tablespoons cold water
salt and pepper

Heat the oil in a large frying pan and fry the chicken, stirring, until beginning to colour. Add the onion and fry until the chicken is golden and the onion softened. Stir in the garlic, then mix in the flour. Add the wine, stock, thyme and a generous sprinkle of salt and pepper. Bring to the boil, stirring, then cover and simmer for 30 minutes.

Heat the butter in a small frying pan, add the mushrooms and fry until golden. Add to the chicken and leave to cool.

Make the pastry. Add the flour, mustard powder and a little salt and pepper to a mixing bowl. Add the fats and rub in with your fingertips or use an electric mixer until you have fine crumbs. Gradually mix in enough of the measured water to form a soft but not sticky dough. Knead lightly, wrap in clingfilm and chill for 15 minutes.

Reserve one-third of the pastry, then cut the rest into 4 pieces. Roll each piece out thinly, then line 4 buttered springform tins, 10 cm (4 inches) in diameter and 4.5 cm (1¾ inches) deep. Roll out the reserved pastry thinly and cut out lids, using the tins as a guide.

Spoon the chicken filling into the pies, brush the top edges with beaten egg, then add the lids and press the pastry edges together. Flute the edges. Bake on a baking sheet in a preheated oven, 190°C (375°F), Gas Mark 5, for 30 minutes until golden. Leave to stand for 5 minutes, then loosen the edges, transfer to a plate and remove the tins. Serve with green vegetables.

Venison &
Red Wine Pie

SERVES 4
PREPARATION TIME 25 minutes
COOKING TIME 2 hours 50 minutes

1 tablespoon olive oil
650 g (1 lb 5 oz) shoulder or
    leg venison, diced
1 onion, chopped
4 streaky bacon rashers, diced
2 garlic cloves, finely chopped
2 tablespoons plain flour
300 ml (½ pint) red wine
450 ml (¾ pint) beef stock
1 tablespoon tomato purée
leaves from 3 rosemary sprigs,
    roughly chopped, plus
    extra, for sprinkling

25 g (1 oz) butter
300 g (10 oz) shallots, halved
    if large
150 g (5 oz) closed-cup
    mushrooms, thickly sliced
1 quantity rosemary
    shortcrust pastry
    (see page 7)
flour, for dusting
beaten egg, to glaze
salt and pepper

Heat the oil in a flameproof casserole, add the venison, then add the onion and bacon, and fry, stirring, until the venison is browned. Stir in the garlic and flour, then mix in the wine, stock and tomato purée. Add the rosemary and season well with salt and pepper.

Bring to the boil, stirring, then cover and transfer to a preheated oven, 160°C (325°F), Gas Mark 3, for 2 hours. Take the dish out of the oven. Heat the butter in a frying pan, add the shallots and mushrooms and fry until golden, then stir into the venison and leave to cool.

Spoon the venison mixture into a 1.2 litre (2 pint) ovenproof pie dish. Roll out the pastry on a lightly floured surface until about 5 cm (2 inches) wider than the diameter of the pie dish. Cut 2 long strips from the edges about 1 cm (½ inch) wide. Brush the dish rim with egg, press the strips on top, then brush these with egg. Lift the pie lid in place, sealing the edges together well. Trim off the excess pastry.

Flute the edge of the pastry. Brush with beaten egg and sprinkle with a few extra torn rosemary leaves. Decorate the top if liked (see page 9). Bake in a preheated oven, 190°C (375°F), Gas Mark 5, for 35–40 minutes until the pastry is golden and the filling piping hot. Serve with green beans and braised red cabbage.

Golden Mushroom & Leek Pies

MAKES 4
PREPARATION TIME 15 minutes
COOKING TIME 25–30 minutes

25 g (1 oz) butter
2 leeks, thinly sliced
300 g (10 oz) chestnut
    mushrooms, quartered
300 g (10 oz) button
    mushrooms, quartered
1 tablespoon plain flour
250 ml (8 fl oz) milk

150 ml (¼ pint) double cream
100 g (3½ oz) mature Cheddar,
    grated
4 tablespoons finely chopped
    parsley
2 sheets of ready-rolled puff
    pastry, defrosted if frozen
beaten egg, to glaze

Melt the butter in a large saucepan, add the leeks and cook for 1–2 minutes. Add the mushrooms and cook for 2 minutes. Stir in the flour and cook, stirring, for 1 minute, then gradually add the milk and cream and cook, stirring constantly, until the mixture thickens. Add the Cheddar and parsley and cook, stirring, for 1–2 minutes. Remove from the heat.

Cut 4 rounds from the pastry sheets to cover each pie dish. Divide the mushroom mixture between the pie dishes. Brush the rims with the beaten egg, then place the pastry rounds on top. Press down around the rims and crimp the edges with a fork. Cut a few of slits in the top of each pie to let the steam out. Brush the pastry with the remaining egg.

Bake in a preheated oven, 220°C (425°F), Gas Mark 7, for 15–20 minutes until the pastry is golden brown.

Serve immediately.

Veg-Forward

Roasted Tomato & Onion Puff Pie

SERVES 4
PREPARATION TIME 20 minutes
COOKING TIME 1 hour

1 kg (2 lb) mixed ripe tomatoes, halved or cut into chunks, depending on size
3 onions, finely sliced
4 garlic cloves, crushed

leaves from 3 oregano sprigs, roughly chopped
3 tablespoons olive oil
320 g (11 oz) ready-rolled vegan puff pastry, defrost if frozen
salt and pepper

Toss together the tomatoes, onions, garlic, oregano, oil and a generous pinch of salt and pepper in a pie dish or roasting tray about 20 x 30 cm (8 x 12 inches). Roast for 30 minutes until the tomatoes are starting to burst and colour.

Lay the puff pastry sheet over the top, press onto the dish or tray edges and trim off any excess. Press around the pastry edges with the tines of a fork to seal. Feel free to make a random pattern with the trimmings and arrange on top of the pastry. Pierce a hole in the centre of the pastry lid with the tip of a knife to allow the steam to escape. Bake in a preheated oven,

190C (375F), gas Mark 5, for 30 minutes until the pastry is golden brown.

Creamy Asparagus Puff Pie

SERVES 6
PREPARATION TIME 25 minutes
COOKING TIME 30–40 minutes

500 g (1 lb) ready-made puff
   pastry, defrosted if frozen
flour, for dusting
beaten egg, to glaze
250 g (8 oz) bunch of
   asparagus
bunch of spring onions
1 tablespoon olive oil

125 g (4 oz) mascarpone
1 large garlic clove, finely
   chopped
25 g (1 oz) Parmesan, grated,
   plus extra for sprinkling
salt and pepper

Roll out the pastry thickly on a lightly floured surface and trim to a 23 × 30 cm (9 × 12 inch) rectangle. Transfer to an oiled baking sheet and use a little beaten egg to glaze. Lightly score a line 2.5 cm (1 inch) in from the edges, then prick the inside rectangle with a fork.

Bake in a preheated oven, 200°C (400°F), Gas Mark 6, for 10 minutes. Press down the centre with the back of a fork, then bake for 5–10 minutes more until the pastry is cooked through. Press down the centre once more.

Meanwhile, trim 2.5 cm (1 inch) from the base of the asparagus, then trim the spring onions to the same length. Toss the asparagus and spring onions in the oil and plenty of salt and pepper, then cook on a preheated ridged frying pan for 5 minutes, turning, until just cooked.

Beat the mascarpone with the garlic, Parmesan, remaining beaten egg and salt and pepper. Spoon into the centre of the pie case and spread into an even layer. Arrange the asparagus and spring onions alternately on top and sprinkle with a little extra Parmesan.

Bake for 10–15 minutes until the filling is just set. Check after 10 minutes and cover with kitchen foil if the pastry seems to be browning too quickly.

Curried Leek & Potato Puffs

MAKES 6
PREPARATION TIME 25 minutes + cooling
COOKING TIME 1 hour–1 hour 15 minutes

500 g (1 lb) floury potatoes, peeled and cut into 2.5 cm (1 inch) cubes

1 leek, thoroughly washed and thickly sliced

3 tablespoons olive oil

75 g (3 oz) frozen peas, defrosted

1 tablespoon lemon or lime juice

1 tablespoon curry powder

500 g (1 lb) puff pastry, defrosted if frozen

flour, for dusting

2 tablespoons milk

1 tablespoon sesame seeds

salt and pepper

Toss the potatoes and leeks with the oil on a large baking tray and season well. Roast in a preheat the oven, 170°C (340°F), Gas Mark 3½, for 30–40 minutes until golden and soft, then leave to cool.

In a medium bowl, lightly mash the roasted leeks and potatoes, leaving some large chunks. Fold in the peas, lemon or lime juice and curry powder. Season and set aside.

On a lightly floured surface, roll out the puff pastry into a large square (about 35 cm / 14 inch). Cut it in half, then cut each half into 3 to give 6 rectangles. Roll each rectangle out a little more to give you a squarer shape of thinner pastry.

Heap 1–2 tablespoons of filling in the centre of each pastry square and fold one corner in diagonally over the filling, making a triangular-shaped pasty. Using your finger or a pastry brush, put some dairy-free milk on the seam to help seal it, push gently with your fingers, then crimp with your fingers or a fork to seal tightly.

Repeat with the remaining pastry squares and filling, then brush all over with dairy-free milk and sprinkle with the sesame seeds.

Place the parcels on a baking tray. Bake in a preheated oven, 190°C (375°F), Gas Mark 5, for 30–35 minutes until puffed and deep golden. Serve warm or at room temperature.

These will keep in the refrigerator for up to 3 days.

Tomato & Olive Bread Pudding

SERVES 4–6
PREPARATION TIME 15 minutes
COOKING TIME 40 minutes + cooling

1 tablespoons olive oil
1 onion, finely sliced
500 g (1 lb) cherry tomatoes, halved
3 garlic cloves, crushed
75 g (3 oz) Kalamata olives, pitted
1 teaspoon cornflour
400 g (13 oz) lightly toasted sourdough bread, torn into smallish chunks
750 ml (1¼ pints) oat milk
salt and pepper
a handful of basil leaves, torn, to garnish

Heat the oil in a shallow ovenproof casserole dish, add the onion and cook for 5 minutes until softened. Then add the tomatoes, garlic and olives and cook for a further 5 minutes. Stir in the cornflour until all the ingredients are coated.

Add the sourdough chunks, season with salt and pepper and pour over the oat milk, then gently stir to combine. Bake in a preheated oven, 200°C (400°F), Gas Mark 6, for 30 minutes until golden.

Leave the pudding to cool for 10 minutes before serving with a scattering of basil.

Wild Mushroom Tart

SERVES 4
PREPARATION TIME 15 minutes + chilling
COOKING TIME 25 minutes

375 g (12 oz) ready-rolled
   shortcrust pastry
2 tablespoons olive oil
1 red onion, sliced
350 g (12 oz) wild and
   chestnut mushrooms,
   trimmed and sliced

2 eggs, beaten
100 g (3½ oz) mascarpone
1 teaspoon thyme leaves
2 teaspoons wholegrain
   mustard
40 g (1½ oz) Parmesan, grated
pepper

Use the pastry to line a 23 cm (9 inch) flan tin. Chill while you make the filling.

Heat the oil in a frying pan and cook the onion and mushrooms for 5 minutes, stirring frequently.

Meanwhile, beat together the eggs, mascarpone and thyme leaves in a bowl and season with pepper.

Add the onion and mushrooms to the egg and mix well.

Spread the mustard over the pastry base. Pour over the filling and level with the back of a spoon.

Sprinkle with the Parmesan. Bake in a preheated oven, 200°C (400°F), Gas Mark 6, for 20 minutes until golden. Slice into generous pieces and serve hot or cold.

Mixed Mushroom Tart

SERVES 6
PREPARATION TIME 45 minutes + chilling & cooling
COOKING TIME 50–55 minutes

FOR THE PASTRY

200 g (7 oz) plain flour, plus
    extra for dusting
½ teaspoon salt
125 g (4 oz) chilled unsalted
    butter, diced
1 egg yolk
2 tablespoons cold water

FOR THE FILLING

50 g (2 oz) butter
6 shallots, finely chopped
2 garlic cloves, crushed
2 teaspoons chopped thyme
350 g (12 oz) mixed
    mushrooms, such as
    shiitake, oyster, brown and
    field, trimmed and sliced
300 ml (½ pint) soured cream
3 eggs, lightly beaten
25 g (1 oz) Parmesan, grated
salt and black pepper

Make the pastry. Sift the flour and salt into a bowl. Add the butter and rub in with your fingertips until the mixture resembles fine breadcrumbs. Add the egg yolk and measured water and bring the mixture together. Wrap in clingfilm and chill for 30 minutes.

Roll the pastry out on a lightly floured work surface. Use to line a 25 cm (10 inch) fluted flan tin. Prick the base with a fork and chill for 30 minutes. Line the pastry with nonstick baking paper and baking beans. Bake in a preheated oven, 200°C (400°F), Gas Mark 6, for 15 minutes. Remove the paper and beans and bake for a further 15 minutes. Leave to cool.

Make the filling. Melt the butter in a frying pan, add the shallots, garlic and thyme and cook over a low heat, stirring frequently, for 5 minutes. Increase the heat, add the mushrooms and salt and pepper and cook, stirring, for 4–5 minutes until browned. Leave to cool. Scatter over the tart case. Beat the soured cream, eggs, Parmesan and a little salt and pepper together and pour over the top. Bake for 20–25 minutes until golden and just set. Serve warm.

Spinach, Pea &
Mint Filo Tart

SERVES 6
PREPARATION TIME 20 minutes + cooling
COOKING TIME 15–20 minutes

FOR THE PESTO

100 g (3½ oz) frozen peas,
   blanched in boiling water
   for 1 minute, then drained
large handful of mint
   (about 30 g / 1¼ oz)
large handful of spinach
   (about 40 g / 1½ oz)
finely grated zest and juice
   of 1 lemon
3 tablespoons extra virgin
   olive oil l
2–3 tablespoons cold water
salt and pepper

FOR THE TART

2 tablespoons olive oil, plus
   extra for brushing
300 g (10 oz) frozen peas,
   defrosted
300 g (10 oz) frozen spinach,
   defrosted and squeezed of
   all excess water
5 spring onions, finely sliced
½ teaspoon freshly grated
   nutmeg
320 g (11 oz) vegan filo
   pastry sheets
leaves from 3 mint sprigs
finely grated zest of 1 lemon
salt and pepper

Make the pesto. Blend all the ingredients together in a food processor until smooth, adding as much of the measured water as you need to loosen the pesto. Season with salt and pepper to taste, and set aside.

Make the tart. Heat the oil in a large frying pan and fry the peas, spinach and spring onions with a pinch of salt over a medium heat until no liquid remains in the pan and the spring onions are soft. Turn off the heat and stir in the pesto, then season with the nutmeg, salt and pepper, and leave to cool

Layer the filo sheets in a large deep baking tin, overlapping each sheet, and brushing each layer with oil, until the whole tin (and its sides) is lined with filo.

Spread the filling evenly across the base, then scrunch up the overhanging pastry to form an edge.

Bake in a preheated oven, 200°C (400°F), Gas Mark 6, for 15 minutes until the filling is firm and the pastry is deep golden brown. Sprinkle with the mint leaves and lemon zest. Serve warm.

Spinach & Pine Nut Tarts

MAKES 6
PREPARATION TIME 25 minutes + chilling
COOKING TIME 27–28 minutes

1 quantity shortcrust pastry
  (see page 7)
flour, for dusting
250 g (8 oz) spinach
25 g (1 oz) butter
1 small onion, finely chopped
2 garlic cloves, finely chopped
¼ teaspoon grated nutmeg
3 eggs
250 ml (8 fl oz) crème fraîche
3 tablespoons pine nuts
salt and pepper

Roll the pastry out thinly on a lightly floured surface and use to line 6 buttered 10 cm (4 inch) fluted loose-bottomed tart tins, rekneading and rerolling the pastry trimmings as needed. Trim off the excess pastry from the top of each tart with scissors so that it stands a little above the tin. Put on a baking sheet and chill for 15 minutes.

Rinse the spinach well, drain in a colander, then dry-fry with just the water clinging to the leaves for 2–3 minutes until the leaves have just wilted. Scoop out of the pan with a slotted spoon, pressing out any excess moisture, then finely chop the leaves.

Drain and dry the pan, then heat the butter and fry the onion for 5 minutes until softened. Stir in the garlic, cook briefly, then return the spinach to the pan. Season with the nutmeg, salt and pepper.

Beat the eggs in a bowl, add the crème fraîche and mix until smooth, then mix with the spinach. Divide between the tarts and sprinkle with the pine nuts.

Bake in a preheated oven, 180°C (350°F), Gas Mark 4, for 20 minutes until the filling is set and the pine nuts are golden. Check after 15 minutes and cover the tops of the tarts loosely with foil if they seem to be browning too quickly. Leave to cool for 5 minutes, then remove from the tins and serve with a green salad.

Creamy Spinach & Egg Tarts

MAKES 4
PREPARATION TIME 15 minutes + chilling
COOKING TIME 19–22 minutes

1 quantity shortcrust pastry
(see page 7)
flour, for dusting
15 g (½ oz) butter
150 g (5 oz) spinach

2 tablespoons double cream
a little grated nutmeg
4 eggs
salt and pepper
grated Cheddar, to serve

Roll the pastry out thinly on a lightly floured surface and use to line 4 buttered 12 cm (5 inch) fluted loose-bottomed tart tins, rekneading and rerolling the pastry trimmings as needed. Trim off the excess pastry with scissors a little above the top of the tin. Prick the bases with a fork, then put on a baking sheet. Chill for 15 minutes.

Heat the butter in a frying pan, add the spinach and cook until just wilted. Mix in the double cream, nutmeg, salt and pepper to taste, and set aside.

Meanwhile bake the tart cases blind (see page 8) in a preheated oven, 190°C (375°F), Gas Mark 5, for 8 minutes. Remove the paper and beans and cook for a further 4 minutes until golden.

Spoon the spinach mixture into the hot pastry cases. Make a dip in the centre, then break an egg into each. Sprinkle with a little more salt and pepper and cook for 5–8 minutes until the egg is to your liking.

Remove the tarts from the tins, transfer to serving plates and sprinkle with the grated cheese. Serve immediately with a green salad.

Feta & Red Pepper Bites

MAKES 18
PREPARATION TIME 25 minutes
COOKING TIME 25–30 minutes

1 tablespoon olive oil, plus extra to serve (optional)
1 onion, thinly sliced
1 garlic clove, finely chopped
125 g (4 oz) ready-roasted red peppers from a jar, drained and thinly sliced
100 g (3½ oz) feta, crumbled

small bunch of thyme
250 g (8 oz) ready-made puff pastry, defrosted if frozen
flour, for dusting
beaten egg, to glaze
9 small stuffed green olives, halved
salt and pepper

Heat the oil in a frying pan, add the onion and fry gently for 10 minutes until soft and just beginning to colour. Add the garlic and peppers and fry for a further 5 minutes until golden. Take the pan off the heat, add the feta, tear leaves from half the thyme over the onion and season with salt and pepper.

Roll the pastry out on a lightly floured surface and trim to a 15 × 30 cm (6 × 12 inch) rectangle, then cut into 5 cm (2 inch) squares. Transfer the squares to an oiled baking sheet, leaving a little space between them.

Brush the tops with beaten egg, then divide the feta mixture between them, and then top with a halved olive.

Bake in a preheated oven, 200°C (400°F), Gas Mark 6, for 10–15 minutes until the pastry is well risen and golden. Brush the olives with a little extra oil, if liked, and sprinkle with the remaining thyme leaves. Serve warm or cold with drinks.

Something Different

Chilli
Corn Bread

MAKES 16
PREPARATION TIME 5 minutes
COOKING TIME 30–35 minutes

150 g (5 oz) rice flour
150 g (5 oz) polenta
1 teaspoon salt
2 teaspoons gluten-free
    baking powder
1 tablespoon caster sugar
3 tablespoons grated
    Parmesan

handful of fresh herbs,
    chopped
1 red chilli, deseeded and
    finely chopped
3 tablespoons olive oil, plus
    extra for oiling
2 eggs, beaten
300 ml (½ pint) buttermilk

Sift the flour, polenta, salt and baking powder into a
large bowl. Stir in the sugar, Parmesan, herbs and chilli.

Mix together the oil, eggs and buttermilk in a separate
bowl, then gently stir into the dry ingredients until
combined.

Tip the mixture into an oiled 20 cm (8inch) square cake
tin. Bake in a preheated oven, 190°C (375°F), Gas Mark 5, for
30–35 minutes until golden. Remove from the oven and
transfer to a wire rack to cool, then cut into 16 squares.
Delicious served with fish chowder. The bread is best eaten
on the same day.

Bacon & Sweetcorn Bread

MAKES 16
PREPARATION TIME 5 minutes
COOKING TIME 30–35 minutes

150 g (5 oz) rice flour
150 g (5 oz) polenta
200 g (7 oz) can sweetcorn, drained
6 bacon rashers, grilled and chopped
1 teaspoon salt
2 teaspoons baking powder
1 tablespoon caster sugar

3 tablespoons grated Parmesan
handful of fresh herbs, chopped
1 red chilli, deseeded and finely chopped
3 tablespoons olive oil, plus extra for oiling
2 eggs, beaten
300 ml (½ pint) buttermilk

Mix the flour, polenta, sweetcorn, bacon, salt and baking powder into a large bowl. Stir in the sugar, Parmesan, herbs and chilli.

Mix the oil, eggs and buttermilk together in a separate bowl, then stir into the flour mixture.

Tip the mixture into an oiled 20 cm (8inch) square cake tin. Bake in a preheated oven, 190°C (375°F), Gas Mark 5, for 30–35 minutes until golden. Remove from the oven and transfer to a wire rack to cool, then cut into 16 squares.

Corn & Bacon Muffins

MAKES 12
PREPARATION TIME 10 minutes
COOKING TIME 20–25 minutes

6 streaky bacon rashers,
   finely chopped
1 small red onion, finely
   chopped
200 g (7 oz) frozen sweetcorn
175 g (6 oz) fine cornmeal
125 g (4 oz) plain flour

2 teaspoons baking powder
50 g (2 oz) Cheddar, grated
200 ml (7 fl oz) milk
2 eggs, beaten
3 tablespoons vegetable oil,
   plus extra for greasing

Heat a frying pan, add the bacon and onion and dry-fry for
3–4 minutes until the bacon is turning crisp.

Cook the sweetcorn in a saucepan of boiling water for
2 minutes to soften. Drain well.

Mix together the cornmeal, flour and baking powder in
a bowl, then stir in the sweetcorn, cheese, bacon and onion.
Mix together the milk, eggs and oil in a separate bowl, add
to the dry ingredients and stir gently to combine.

Pour the mixture into the greased holes of a 12-hole
muffin tray. Bake in a preheated oven, 220°C (425°F), Gas
Mark 7, for 15–20 minutes until golden and just firm to the
touch. Remove from the oven and transfer to a wire rack
to cool.

Herbed
Soda Breads

MAKES 8
PREPARATION TIME 10 minutes
COOKING TIME 25–30 minutes

250 g (8 oz) wholemeal flour,
plus extra for dusting
250 g (8 oz) plain flour
1 teaspoon bicarbonate
of soda
1 teaspoon salt
50 g (2 oz) butter, chilled and
diced, plus extra for
greasing

1 spring onion, finely chopped
1 tablespoon chopped parsley
1 tablespoon chopped thyme
1 tablespoon chopped
rosemary
275 ml (9 fl oz) buttermilk

Sift the flours, bicarbonate of soda and salt into a bowl. Add the butter and rub in with your fingertips until the mixture resembles fine breadcrumbs. Add the spring onion and herbs and mix well to combine. Make a well in the centre and add the buttermilk. Mix with a round-bladed knife to make a soft dough.

Turn out on to a lightly floured work surface and knead lightly into a ball. Divide the dough between 8 greased dariole moulds.

Place the dariole moulds on a baking sheet, flatten the dough slightly and dust with flour.

Bake in a preheated oven, 220°C (425°F), Gas Mark 7, for 25–30 minutes until risen, golden and hollow sounding when tapped underneath. Transfer to a wire rack to cool. For a softer crust, wrap the hot breads in a clean tea towel to cool. Eat the same day.

Herb & Cheese Damper

SERVES 8
PREPARATION TIME 10 minutes
COOKING TIME 30 minutes

500 g (1 lb) self-raising flour,
  plus extra for dusting
½ teaspoon salt
15 g (½ oz) chilled butter, diced
50 g (2 oz) Cheddar, grated

2 teaspoons chopped
  rosemary
150 ml (¼ pint) milk
150 ml (¼ pint) water
spray oil, for oiling

Sift the flour and salt into a bowl. Add the butter and rub in with your fingertips until the mixture resembles fine breadcrumbs. Stir in the Cheddar and rosemary. Make a well in the centre, add the milk and measured water and gradually work into the flour mixture to form a soft dough.

Turn the dough out on a lightly floured work surface and knead gently into a smooth ball. Transfer the dough to a lightly oiled baking sheet and flatten slightly to form an 18 cm (7 inch) round. Using a sharp knife, score the surface into 8 wedges. Bake in a preheated oven, 200°C (400°F), Gas Mark 6, for about 30 minutes until risen and the loaf sounds hollow when tapped underneath. Transfer to a wire rack and leave to cool completely.

For individual rolls, divide the dough into 8 pieces. Shape each piece into a ball and flatten slightly into a round. Brush each one with a little milk and scatter over a little extra grated Cheddar. Bake at 200°C (400°F), Gas Mark 6, for 18–20 minutes.

Caribbean Chicken Patties

MAKES 4
PREPARATION TIME 30 minutes + chilling
COOKING TIME 30–35 minutes

FOR THE FILLING
2 tablespoons sunflower oil
250 g (8 oz) boneless, skinless chicken breast, diced
250 g (8 oz) butternut squash, peeled, deseeded and diced
1 small onion, chopped
2 garlic cloves, finely chopped
½ small hot bonnet chilli, deseeded and finely chopped
1 red or orange pepper, deseeded and diced
1 teaspoon mild curry powder or paste
2 tablespoons chopped coriander
beaten egg, to glaze
pepper

FOR THE PASTRY
250 g (8 oz) plain flour, plus extra for dusting
1½ teaspoons turmeric
125 g (4 oz) white vegetable fat, diced
2½–3 tablespoons cold water
salt

Make the pastry. Add the flour, turmeric, fat and a little salt to a mixing bowl, and rub the fat in with your fingertips or use an electric mixer until you have fine crumbs. Gradually mix in enough of the measured water to form a soft but not sticky dough. Knead lightly, then wrap in clingfilm and chill.

Make the filling. Heat the oil in a frying pan, add the chicken and butternut squash and fry for 5 minutes until the chicken is just beginning to brown. Add the onion, garlic, chilli and pepper and fry for 5 minutes until the vegetables are softened and the chicken cooked through. Add the curry powder, coriander and a little pepper and cook briefly, then take off the heat and leave to cool.

Cut the pastry into 4 pieces, roll each piece out on a lightly floured surface and trim to an 18 cm (7 inch) circle. Divide the filling between the pastry circles, brush the edges with beaten egg, then fold in half and press the edges together well, first with your fingertips, then with the prongs of a fork, until well sealed.

Transfer to an oiled baking sheet and brush the patties with beaten egg. Bake in a preheated oven, 190°C (375°F), Gas Mark 5, for 20–25 minutes. Serve hot or cold with chilli tomato chutney.

Cheesy Potato, Garlic & Chive Cakes

MAKES 6
PREPARATION TIME 10 minutes
COOKING TIME 15 minutes

250 g (8 oz) potato, peeled and cut into 1.5 cm (¾ inch) cubes
25 g (1 oz) butter, plus extra for cooking
50 g (2 oz) rice flour, plus extra for dusting
1 teaspoon baking powder
75 g (3 oz) Cheshire cheese, crumbled
1 garlic clove, crushed
1 teaspoon chopped chives
2 tablespoons buttermilk
1 egg, beaten
vegetable oil, for brushing
salt

Cook the potatoes in a saucepan of salted boiling water for 10 minutes, or until tender. Drain well.

Place the potato and butter in a large bowl and mash together until smooth, then stir in the remaining ingredients together with a pinch of salt until combined. Bring the mixture together to form a ball.

Turn the dough out on a floured surface and roll to 5 mm (¼ inch) thick, then cut out 6 rounds.

Brush a nonstick frying pan with a little oil and add a knob of butter, then cook the cakes for 2–3 minutes on each side until golden. Serve warm with butter.

Potato & Thyme
Griddle Scones

MAKES 6
PREPARATION TIME 10 minutes
COOKING TIME 15 minutes

250 g (8 oz) potato, peeled
and cut into 1.5 cm (¾ inch)
cubes

25 g (1 oz) butter, plus extra
for cooking

50 g (2 oz) rice flour, plus extra
for dusting

1 teaspoon baking powder

1 teaspoon chopped thyme,
plus extra sprigs to garnish
(optional)

2 tablespoons buttermilk

1 egg, beaten

vegetable oil, for brushing

salt

Cook the potatoes in a saucepan of salted boiling water for
10 minutes, or until tender. Drain well.

Place the potato and butter in a large bowl and mash
together until smooth, then stir in the remaining ingredients
together with a pinch of salt until combined. Bring the
mixture together to form a ball.

Turn the dough out on a floured surface and roll to 5 mm
(¼ inch) thick, then cut out 6 triangles.

Brush a griddle or frying pan with a little oil and add a
little butter, then cook the scones for 2–3 minutes on each
side until golden. Serve warm with butter and cheese.

Cheese &
Matcha Scones

MAKES 6
PREPARATION TIME 20 minutes
COOKING TIME 12 minutes

450 g (14½ oz) self-raising flour,
plus extra for dusting
1 teaspoon sea salt
1 tablespoon matcha powder
100 g (3½ oz) chilled unsalted
butter, cut into small cubes

250 g (8 oz) mature Cheddar,
finely grated
120 ml (4 fl oz) cold milk or
buttermilk
120 ml (4 fl oz) cold water
1 egg, beaten with a splash
of milk

Put the flour, salt and matcha powder into a large bowl and mix together until well combined. Add the butter and rub it into the flour with your fingertips until it looks grainy.

Add 225 g (7½ oz) of the cheese and stir to combine. Mix in the milk and measured water, until the dough just comes away from the side of the bowl. Transfer to a lightly floured surface and flatten the dough into a rectangle about 2.5 cm (1 inch) thick. Using a sharp knife, cut into 6 large triangles. Gently push any offcuts together to cut more shapes.

Transfer the dough to a baking tray lined with baking paper and brush with the egg and milk mixture. Sprinkle the remaining cheese over the tops. Bake in a preheated oven, 220°C (425°F), Gas Mark 7, for 12 minutes, or until golden. Transfer to a wire rack to cool before serving.

Garlic & Caramelized Onion Bhajis

MAKES 6
PREPARATION TIME 10 minutes + standing
COOKING TIME 15 minutes

2 tablespoons olive oil
1 onion, sliced
2 garlic cloves, sliced
1 teaspoon cumin seeds
2 tablespoons chopped
    coriander

200 g (7 oz) gram flour
1 teaspoon bicarbonate
    of soda
½ teaspoon salt
250 ml (8 fl oz) water

Heat half the oil in a nonstick frying pan, add the onion,
garlic and cumin and fry for 5–6 minutes until the onion
is golden and softened. Stir in the coriander.

Meanwhile, mix together the flour, bicarbonate of soda,
salt and measured water in a bowl and set aside to rest for
10 minutes, then stir in the onion mixture.

Heat a little of the remaining oil in the frying pan, add
spoonfuls of the onion mixture and fry for 2–3 minutes,
turning halfway through cooking. Transfer to a serving
plate and keep warm while frying the remainder of the
mixture. Serve warm with mint chutney or thick natural
yogurt to dip.

Spicy Spinach & Onion Bhajis

MAKES 6
PREPARATION TIME 10 minutes + standing
COOKING TIME 15 minutes

2 tablespoons olive oil
1 onion, sliced
2 garlic cloves, sliced
1 teaspoon cumin seeds
75 g (3 oz)spinach, cooked,
    well squeezed and
    chopped

2 tablespoons chopped
    coriander
200 g (7 oz) gram flour
1 teaspoon bicarbonate
    of soda
½ teaspoon dried chilli flakes
½ teaspoon salt
250 ml (8 fl oz) water

Heat half the oil in a nonstick frying pan, add the onion, garlic and cumin and fry for 5–6 minutes until the onion is golden and softened. Stir in the spinach and coriander.

Meanwhile, mix together the flour, bicarbonate of soda, chilli, salt and measured water in a bowl and set aside for 10 minutes, then stir in the onion and spinach mixture.

Heat a little of the remaining oil in the frying pan, add spoonfuls of the spinach mixture and fry for 2–3 minutes, turning halfway through cooking. Transfer to a serving plate and keep warm while frying the remainder of the mixture. Serve warm with mint chutney.

Mexican Egg Tarts

MAKES 4
PREPARATION TIME 25 minutes + chilling
COOKING TIME 25–28 minutes

1 quantity shortcrust pastry
  (see page 7)
flour, for dusting
1 tablespoon olive oil
1 onion, chopped
1 red pepper, cored, deseeded
  and diced
75 g (3 oz) chorizo, diced
2 garlic cloves, finely chopped
¼ teaspoon smoked paprika

2 bay leaves
200 g (7 oz) can chopped
  tomatoes
150 g (5 oz) cherry tomatoes,
  halved
4 eggs
salt and pepper
a few tiny basil leaves
  (optional)
grated Cheddar, to serve

Cut the pastry into 4 pieces, then roll each piece out on a lightly floured surface until a little larger than a buttered 12 cm (5 inch) fluted loose-bottomed tart tin. Lift the pastry into the tins, then press over the base and sides. Trim off the excess pastry with scissors a little above the top of the tin. Prick the bases with a fork, then put on a baking sheet. Chill for 15 minutes.

Heat the oil in a saucepan, add the onion, red pepper and chorizo and fry for 5 minutes until softened. Stir in the garlic, paprika and bay leaves, then add the canned tomatoes and season with salt and pepper. Simmer gently, uncovered for 15 minutes, stirring from time to time until thickened. Discard the bay leaves.

Meanwhile bake the tarts blind (see page 8) for 8 minutes. Remove the paper and beans and cook for a further 4 minutes until golden.

Stir the cherry tomatoes into the hot sauce and spoon into the hot pastry cases. Make a dip in the centre, then break an egg into each. Sprinkle with salt and pepper and cook for 5–8 minutes until the egg is to your liking.

Remove the tarts from the tins, transfer to serving plates, sprinkle with basil leaves, if liked, grated cheese and serve with a green salad.

Curried Sausage Rolls

MAKES 30
PREPARATION TIME 30 minutes
COOKING TIME 20 minutes

500 g (1 lb) good-quality pork
   sausage meat
50 g (2 oz) sultanas
5 cm (2 inch) root ginger,
   peeled and coarsely grated
2 garlic cloves, chopped
2 tablespoons coriander,
   chopped
1 teaspoon turmeric

1 teaspoon black peppercorns,
   roughly crushed
500 g (1 lb) ready-made puff
   pastry, defrosted if frozen
flour, for dusting
beaten egg, to glaze
3 teaspoons mild curry paste
salt

Add the sausage meat, sultanas, ginger, garlic and coriander to a large bowl, sprinkle over the turmeric, pepper and a little salt, then mix together with a wooden spoon or your hands.

Roll the pastry out thinly on a lightly floured surface and trim to a 30 cm (12 inch) square. Cut the square into 3 strips, 10 cm (4 inches) wide, then brush lightly with beaten egg. Spread 1 teaspoon of curry paste in a band down the centre of each pastry strip, then top each strip with one-third of the sausage meat mixture, spooning into a narrow band.

Fold the pastry over the filling and press the edges together well with the flattened tip of a small sharp knife. Trim the edge to neaten if needed, then slash the top of the strips.

Brush the sausage rolls with beaten egg, then cut each strip into 10 pieces and arrange slightly spaced apart on 2 lightly oiled baking sheets. Cook in a preheated oven, 200°C (400°F), Gas Mark 6, for about 20 minutes until golden and the pastry is well risen. Transfer to a wire rack and leave to cool for 20 minutes. Serve warm or cold.

Mini Harissa Sausage Rolls

MAKES 30
PREPARATION TIME 30 minutes
COOKING TIME 20 minutes

500 g (1 lb) good-quality pork
sausage meat
50 g (2 oz) walnut pieces,
roughly chopped
5 cm (2 inch) root ginger,
peeled and coarsely grated

1 teaspoon black peppercorns,
roughly crushed
500 g (1 lb) ready-made puff
pastry, defrosted if frozen
flour, for dusting
beaten egg, to glaze
3 teaspoons harissa paste
salt

Add the sausage meat, walnuts and ginger to a large bowl, sprinkle over the pepper and a little salt, then mix together with a wooden spoon or your hands.

Roll the pastry out thinly on a lightly floured surface and trim to a 30 cm (12 inch) square. Cut the square into 3 strips, 10 cm (4 inches) wide, then brush lightly with beaten egg. Spread 1 teaspoon of harissa in a band down the centre of each pastry strip, then top each strip with one-third of the sausage meat mixture, spooning into a narrow band.

Fold the pastry over the filling and press the edges together well with the flattened tip of a small sharp knife. Trim the edge to neaten if needed, then slash the top of the strips.

Brush the sausage rolls with beaten egg, then cut each strip into 10 pieces and arrange slightly spaced apart on 2 lightly oiled baking sheets. Cook in a preheated oven, 200°C (400°F), Gas Mark 6, for about 20 minutes until golden and the pastry is well risen. Transfer to a wire rack and leave to cool for 20 minutes. Serve warm or cold.

Asian-Style Mushroom Parcels

MAKES 4
PREPARATION TIME 25 minutes
COOKING TIME 25 minutes

4 large field mushrooms, wiped
1 tablespoon sesame oil
1 tablespoon ketjap manis or soy sauce
2.5 cm (1 inch) root ginger, peeled and finely chopped
2 garlic cloves, finely chopped
4 tablespoons roughly chopped coriander
1 tomato, cut into 4 thick slices
25 g (1 oz) butter, cut into 4 pieces
1 quantity shortcrust pastry (see page 7)
flour, for dusting
beaten egg, to glaze
4 teaspoons sesame seeds, for sprinkling
pepper

Trim the top of the mushroom stalks level with the caps, drizzle the gills with the sesame oil and ketjap manis or soy sauce, then sprinkle with the ginger, garlic and coriander. Top each with a slice of tomato, a piece of butter and a little pepper.

Cut the pastry into 4 pieces, roll out one piece thinly on a lightly floured surface to a 18–20 cm (7–8 inch) circle, or large enough to enclose the mushrooms (this will depend on how big they are, so make a little bigger if needed).

Place a mushroom on top of a pastry circle, brush the edges with beaten egg, then lift the pastry up and over the top of the mushroom, pleating the pastry as you go and pinching the ends together in the centre of the mushroom to completely enclose it. Repeat to make 4 parcels and put them onto a buttered baking sheet.

Brush the parcels with beaten egg and sprinkle with the sesame seeds. Bake in a preheated oven, 200°C (400°F), Gas Mark 6, for about 25 minutes until golden brown. Transfer to serving plates and accompany with stir-fried vegetables and soy sauce.

Gingered Prawn Samosas

MAKES 18
PREPARATION TIME 30 minutes
COOKING TIME 35–45 minutes

FOR THE FILLING
2 medium baking potatoes, about 300 g (10 oz), scrubbed
2 tablespoons sunflower oil
1 onion, finely chopped
1½ teaspoons black mustard seeds
2 teaspoons cumin seeds, roughly crushed
2.5 cm (1 inch) root ginger, peeled and grated
2 Thai green chillies, with seeds, finely chopped
1 teaspoon coriander seeds, crushed

3 tablespoons chopped coriander
¼ teaspoon turmeric
100 g (3½ oz) small cooked peeled prawns, defrosted if frozen
75 g (3 oz) frozen peas, defrosted
salt and pepper
1 litre sunflower oil, for deep-frying

FOR THE PASTRY
200 g (7 oz) plain flour
50 g (2 oz) butter or ghee, diced
4–5 tablespoons cold water
salt

Make the filling. Cook the potatoes whole in boiling water for 15–20 minutes until tender. Drain and leave until cool enough to handle, then peel off the skins and dice the flesh.

Heat the oil in the drained and dried potato pan, add the onion and fry for 3 minutes, then add the mustard seeds, cumin seeds, ginger and chillies and cook for 2 minutes. Mix in the crushed and chopped coriander, turmeric, then the potatoes, prawns, peas and plenty of salt and pepper.

Make the pastry. Add the flour, a little salt and the butter or ghee to a mixing bowl. Rub in the butter with your fingertips until you have fine crumbs, then mix in enough of the measured water to form a soft but not sticky dough. Knead well until smooth and elastic. Cut into 9 pieces and shape into balls. Roll out to 12 cm (5 inch) circles.

Cut each circle in half, brush the edges with water, then shape into a cone by folding one point to the centre of the curved top; do the same with the other point. Spoon the filling into the cone, then press the curved edges together to seal. Repeat to make 18 samosas.

Half-fill a large saucepan with oil, heat to 180°C (350°F) on a sugar thermometer, or until the oil bubbles when a samosa is lowered into the oil. Cook the samosas in batches of 3 or 4 for 3–4 minutes until golden brown, then lift out using a slotted spoon and transfer to a plate lined with kitchen paper. Serve warm with mango chutney or cucumber raita.

Recipes Index

Recipes are marked as
being suitable for vegans
(vg) or vegetarians (v)

UK/US Glossary

aubergine ....eggplant

baking tray ....baking sheet

beetroot ....beets

cake tin ....cake pan

chilli ....chili

chilli flakes ....red pepper flakes

clingfilm ....plastic wrap

coriander ....cilantro

cornflour ....cornstarch

courgette .... zucchini

cream (double) .... heavy cream

flour (plain) ....all-purpose

flour (self-raising) ....self-rising

flour (wholemeal) ....whole-wheat

frying pan ....skillet

grill ....broil

jug .... pitcher

kitchen paper .... paper towels

natural yogurt ....plain yogurt

pastry case ....pie case

pepper (green/red/yellow) ....

....bell pepper

porridge oats ....oatmeal

prawn ....shrimp

rocket .... arugula

sieve ....strainer

spring onion ....scallion

sugar (caster) ....superfine

sweetcorn ....corn

tart ....pie

tomato purée ....tomato paste

Publisher's note:

Standard level spoon measurements are used in all recipes.

1 tablespoon = one 15 ml spoon
1 teaspoon = one 5 ml spoon

Both imperial and metric measurements have been given in all recipes. Use one set of measurements only and not a mixture of both.

Eggs should be medium unless otherwise stated. The Department of Health advises that eggs should not be consumed raw. This book contains dishes made with raw or lightly cooked eggs. It is prudent for more vulnerable people such as pregnant and nursing mothers, the elderly, babies and young children to avoid uncooked or lightly cooked dishes made with eggs. Once prepared these dishes should be kept refrigerated and used promptly.

Milk should be full fat unless otherwise stated.

Fresh herbs should be used unless otherwise stated. If unavailable use dried herbs as an alternative but halve the quantities stated.

Ovens should be preheated to the specific temperature – if using a fan-assisted oven, follow manufacturer's instructions for adjusting the time and the temperature.

Pepper should be freshly ground black pepper unless otherwise stated.

This book includes dishes made with nuts and nut derivatives. It is advisable for customers with known allergic reactions to nuts and nut derivatives and those who may be potentially vulnerable to these allergies, such as babies and children with a family history of allergies, to avoid dishes made with nuts and nut oils. It is also prudent to check the labels of pre-prepared ingredients for the possible inclusion of nut derivatives.

Vegetarians should look for the 'V' symbol on a cheese to ensure it is made with vegetarian rennet.

Also Available

Recipes for Pickling & Preserving

Recipes for Soups

Recipes for Summer